Praise

"Manoj has shared some of the most meaningful life experiences and has unfolded various financial tools in a step by step method to explain a complex and most sought after subject called Financial Freedom.

This book is an outstanding attempt to make your dreams come true and achieve inner happiness. It touches every aspect of financial planning and makes it one of the finest books ever written with examples, recommendation and experiences."

Ashok Monga,
Joint General Manager,
Head—Corporate Social Responsibility,
Larsen & Toubro Ltd.

"… Most of the limiting factors to our financial success exist in the walls we all have built up : our own minds, and achieving success lies in knocking down those walls.

Manoj has beautifully converted this idea into the book …, this book is not only strong on the actual mechanics of personal finance, but its other major strength is in setting the psychological stage for strong personal finance habits.

Another distinct feature of this book is the heavily anecdotal nature of the book. Manoj likes to use lots of anecdotes to illustrate the points – and he's pretty good at choosing truly strong ones. These anecdotes emphasize on the psychological underpinnings of a thought process."

Sandeep Sehgal,
Founder, Director and CEO,
Pallas Athena Consulting Pvt. Ltd.

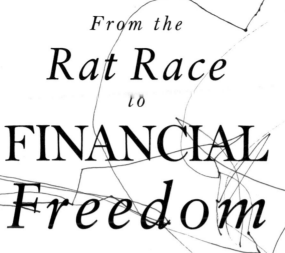

From the
Rat Race
to
FINANCIAL
Freedom

A common man's journey...

MANOJ ARORA

JAICO PUBLISHING HOUSE

Ahmedabad Bangalore Bhopal Bhubaneswar Chennai
Delhi Hyderabad Kolkata Lucknow Mumbai

Published by Jaico Publishing House
A-2 Jash Chambers, 7-A Sir Phirozshah Mehta Road
Fort, Mumbai - 400 001
jaicopub@jaicobooks.com
www.jaicobooks.com

© Manoj Arora

FROM THE RAT RACE TO FINANCIAL FREEDOM
ISBN 978-81-8495-400-5

First Jaico Impression: 2013

Page design and layouts: Special Effects, Mumbai

Printed by
Concept Imprint Pvt. Ltd.
Plot No. 51/1/4, Site IV, Industrial Area
Sahibabad, Ghaziabad - 201010 (UP)

Contents

Preface

Choose your Life!!

Our lives are a sum total of the choices we have made.
— **Wayne Dyer**

When you have to make a choice and don't make it,
that is in itself a choice.
— **Anonymous**

Here is an extract from the speech that I made during one of the leadership seminars on 22nd Nov 2007 after I joined IBM India as a software testing manager in 2006.

This was when my dream of financial freedom was just surfacing. I was never and am still not a very good speaker but since this was one of my favourite topics, I felt very comfortable speaking in front of a large audience that day.

I AM A FREE MAN

This is the day I have been waiting and planning for a long time now!!! I am excited and thrilled that I have achieved the biggest goal of my life – to be a full time father, husband and son..... YES I HAVE DONE IT!!!!

My kids will go to tuitions! No way!!.......... I am there to guide them throughout as I am available for them 24X7. I am there to tell them not 1 but 10 stories in a day. I am there with them in the park playing badminton and tennis with them ... only on Sundays...NO... on any day THEY choose! My kids go to school in a school bus!! No Way!!!! I am the only father to drive them to school...not on the day when they are late for school... but everyday... Of course I missed their chit chat all through those years when I had to go to office and they had to go in their school bus. We are now sharing our dreams together!!!

My wife has finally got a full time husband and my parents a full time son!! My parents need not go for their routine checkups in a taxi, auto or a bus...they have a full time driver at their disposal — their son. My wife needs to go for shopping and don't you think

I love shopping too!!! We go together for shopping while the kids are at school

What do you think? Am I retired by age? No!! I am financially free!! I can do what I want… what my family wants!! My family does not see Hollywood and my kids do not see Disneyland only on TV now! We are right there to experience it live!!

Today, I write this sitting at the side of my private pool with a beer mug in my hand. But you know what the best part is!! I don't have to go to office tomorrow!!… because I have earned enough to be financially free!!! I can sit and enjoy here as long as I like to.

Yes, I had my share of pains and struggle to reach where I am today. But today I realize that every bit of it was worth the effort. I see a world of no EMIs, no Credit Cards, and no forced jobs where I am ready to experience and enjoy my long forgotten hobbies…. Now I will start learning Guitar … a hobby I started and left many years back. I have to enroll my wife and myself in Salsa learning classes ….. We love to dance, yes we do!!

The satisfaction I get today is not only the freedom of money but also the freedom of Time and the string of choices that they bring along with them.

I AM A FREE MAN

There was a huge round of applause as I ended this speech. But more than the round of applause, I was happier seeing the cheerful faces of the audience. I have given such leadership talks many times and I know that most of the time it is customary to applaud the speaker. But the cheer and smile on the faces of the audience told a completely different story. I was becoming more and more convinced that we are missing this in our lives. If the mere thought and a five minute journey to personal freedom could take the audience to such levels of bliss and happiness, I could imagine what living that goal could do to them.

Most people in the audience could relate to the passion and emotion in my speech, and what freedom could bring to their own lives, if they could somehow achieve it. Someone was needed to show them the path.

Why did I share this with you?

To make you realize that even a common person like you and me has a right to dream and transform that dream into reality. Doubtless, it does need planning, discipline, commitment and sacrifice, but "it is possible". It is a choice and we can make that choice.

I will be the first person to tell you that I definitely love money and also the first one to ask you – Who does not love money?

I am here to tell you that you can go on to enjoy the beauty of financial freedom irrespective of what stage of life you are in today or the present financial status of your portfolio. Financial freedom is within the reach of each one of us.

But before we get into how to go about achieving this, let us understand what we expect money to do for us.

What do you really want from money? Why are you striving so hard to get the next promotion in your company, the next salary raise, the next order for your newly started business? Why are you ready to sacrifice moments of family happiness for the teleconference that you have with your client? Why?

Ultimately, it is all to bring in more money. But what do you want to do with that additional money that often comes at the cost of your health, family and friends. Why do you want to be financially independent? Is it the new car that you want to buy, the new apartment that attracts you? Do you want to travel and see the world? Or is it that you simply want to spend more time with your family and children? What is it? When I asked myself these simple but logical questions, I had a big tussle going on in my mind till I reached a satisfactory answer.

"Wouldn't it be great to have enough money so that you don't have to worry?"

Lack of money causes so many worries in our life with regards to our future that this can be a very simple and strong reason to have enough money with you and become financially free. Once you reach that stage, you can actually start doing what you want to do in life. And stop cursing your boss, company, parents, society, country and politicians for the state of financial dependency you have always been in. This is what I truly term as financial freedom. It takes the worry out of your life and allows you to do what you enjoy the most. This could be trivial things like planting trees, teaching underprivileged children, spending time to teach your own children or just helping out your relatives, neighbours, society, country or the world.

There is no part of our life that money does not touch. It affects our relationships, the way we go about every day activities of our lives, our ability to make our dreams a reality, in fact everything!! The fact that money does not buy happiness is a very true statement, but money does enable you to create more happiness in life if you know how to do so. I do not know if I have discovered the true meaning of life yet but I have already learnt a great deal about what money can do.

As someone said:
"It's not the knife which kills; it's the intention of the person holding the knife that kills."

A knife can solve so many of your complex problems in the kitchen if you know how to take care while using it and if you have the right intent to use it.

Likewise, money can do wonders if you know how to take care of your money and if you have the right intent. If you have some goals in life for which you wish to take out more time, money can definitely help you buy that time.

My career blasted off with a gold medal and a campus selection in L&T after passing my Engineering degree from Aligarh Muslim University. Having served the industry for almost 6 years, I made a push towards the IT industry. "This was the master move" I thought to myself. And it turned out to be so, starting off from a small IT firm, I jumped jobs and saw my salary go up almost 10 times in the next 9 years and had the pleasure of working for some of the Fortune 500 organizations like TCS and IBM.

Along with my professional life, my personal life was running on a parallel track and going equally well. God was very kind to us. By this time, I had two beautiful, adorable and charming daughters. My life seemed to be ideal –the successful story of a smart, modern IT professional.

But as may be the case with most of us (it is a separate fact that we may or may not agree), my wife and I were still not happy from within. We still had the fear of losing our jobs, and losing our monthly pay cheques. We feared what would happen to us in case we were to lose our jobs. Our children were definitely a priority for us.

My wife decided to quit her job to take care of the children. Our family was now dependent on my single source of income. The more I grew in my career, the more unstable the entire system holding our personal and professional life became. As time passed by and I grew in my career, I knew that something else was growing with the same momentum, if not more – the fear of falling down like a pack of cards.

My job was taking up a major part of my time and my life. It was becoming a higher priority, than my spouse, my children, my parents and even myself. I have been part of many coffee table discussions, during my long career, with the best of the best in the IT industry. It is an irony and also a fact that so many of so called "successful professionals" take pride in sharing some seemingly strange facts. I want to reproduce a few of them as I am sure you will be able to relate with some of them.

"I worked even when my kids were sick;" "I attended a meeting an hour after the funeral of my dad," and some felt a sense of pride in saying that *"I did not take a single holiday in the last 3 years"* or *"I only saw my children growing horizontally in their beds."*

The list of such "proud" expressions is endless. I never understood the logic in any of them. I am not advocating that you be unfaithful to your company or to your work, I am only trying to say that you should keep the larger perspective in mind before taking any decision.

My simple question to myself whenever I heard such statements, was "Are these people earning money to live or are they living to earn money?"

In a competitive environment where we have to depend so much on someone else's opinion about us, the whole purpose of money seems to have been lost somewhere. It has taken priority over our relations in every sphere of life. Was that the purpose of money? Was money supposed to be an "end" by itself or a "means" to achieve the goals of life? It was definitely not the former. It took me time and brainstorming to realize that. It might take you some time as well, but it is worth every minute that you spend on this aspect.

I also wanted to earn lots of money. Not that I was in a race to have more money but I wanted money to make me financially free so that I could pursue my real dreams and goals of life. And as it is said, if you are really looking for something, the entire universe will conspire to help you get it.

I was looking out. I was shown a network marketing business. I am sure many of you have heard the name of Amway. Different people in different countries and cultures have different views about the network marketing (multi level marketing) business. It is definitely not held in high esteem by most people. Well, I was now into it and the only thing that drove me into this network marketing business and also drove me to build this business were some of the popular phrases that I heard people using in this business, some of these terms — I had never heard earlier in my school, college or my job.

I was hearing words like "passive income", "retirement", "live your dreams", and many more such words and phrases which struck a chord with me somewhere. While I invested a lot of time and energy in Amway, I was moving even farther away from my friends and family, in the lure of ultimately becoming financially independent and being able to spend more quality time with my parents, wife and children.

After giving 3 years of my valuable time, effort and money to this network marketing business, I quit it in 2007. The business taught me some of the most important lessons of my life, which ultimately became "the turning point" in my life. As it is said, everything that happens to you has a definite purpose. I clearly knew why I had joined this business, though I quit it without being successful. I knew it had given me what I wanted. It had given me my dreams and goals. I now had big dreams and big goals to achieve in life, courtesy Amway. I knew what I wanted to achieve.

After I left Amway in 2007 I started a slow but steady process of gaining more knowledge on financial freedom and slowly worked on a month on month personal financial plan which, I will share with you in the later sections of this book along with all the learning I gained on my journey towards financial freedom.

Finally, the most important thing, I will share with you how this financial independence helped me achieve what I always wanted to achieve in life – resigning from my job, planting trees and educating underprivileged children in our society.

Initially when I started I did not know where life would take me from here, how many more goals would emerge as I went along and how I would achieve some of the existing ones. Believe me, the satisfaction of "giving" to others seems to be becoming the purpose of my life. How has money contributed to this? It has given me the time and freedom to opt out of the rat race and go ahead and execute my plans, because "I don't have to worry about my monthly salary to survive."

Whatever your goal is, you can always make it happen. Step by step, you can take charge of your destiny and achieve financial independence. The power is within you.

The road to financial independence does not begin in a bank or a financial planner's office but in your head. It begins with your thoughts. And if you have taken some time to read this book, let me tell you that you have just taken the first step. I will take you through that journey with me. I can guide you, help you but your dream has to drive you!

Never give up on your true dreams in life, thinking that they are difficult; or that no one has ever succeeded in them earlier; or how will you achieve them; or what will people say if you do what you dream.

Keep dreaming…it's the first step to their realization.

A former president of India and one of the most respected and renowned Indian personalities worldwide once said…

Dream… Dream… and Dream…

Dream creates thoughts,
Thoughts create your actions
And actions create your destiny!

*~ **Dr. Abdul Kalam***

Introduction

Why should you read this book...?

All around us the story is the same inflation — economic mess. It does not matter whether you have a job, run a shop or are a small, medium or a big entrepreneur. Each one of us is stuck in a mindless rat race[5]. I was no different. I was running, not knowing where I was headed. Worse, even though I realized that this was a mindless race, I did not seem to have a solution to this aimless and missionless competition.

Was there a need to come out of this race? Was there a way to come out of this race? What would I do with my life if I could somehow come out of it? These were some of the questions crisscrossing my mind during the first half of my 20 year long career as an electrical engineer and then as an IT professional working for some of the best companies across the globe.

It took 10 years in these high profile jobs for me to crystallize my dreams and reach the conclusion that life has to be much more than competing by pulling others down, getting salary increments, promotions, progressions and raising a family. I was somehow able to convince myself that God did not send us to this lovely planet just for this. While earning money was as important as raising one's family, this could not be the end of your life's achievements and goals. I spent enough time and effort on myself to crystallize my life goals – goals that could give me "true happiness."

Whatever my goals, the fundamental question that lay in front of me was how am I going to achieve these goals if I am stuck in a race which never seems to end. Where would I get the time and money to accomplish these goals?

I was working in a job that became more and more demanding every day. Yes, I was getting a better position and better salary each year but guess what; I still could not seem to save "enough." Where was all the money going? What was happening? I had a better car, better house, and better furniture but why was I not as happy as I was when I was younger? Where had my happiness gone? How long could I continue to do this? What if something happened to me and I was out of work for a few months? How would my family survive? Why was I still struggling to survive after so many years of a "successful" career? How would I ever be able to get out of this trap and even think about my life goals – goals that go beyond the six individuals in my family?

As all these questions were haunting me, I realized that the first logical step to achieving my true life goals had to be evading this trap of earning money. There had to be a way. And once I was out of this trap, then I could truly pursue the other cherished goals of my life. Life without these goals, only ends in frustration and unfulfilled desires.

This book takes you through the journey of how I managed to break free from this trap and became a financially free individual. It documents all my learning and experience during this beautiful journey. Only 1% of the people in the world are successfully able to finish this journey and I know I am one of those special ones.

Is this journey difficult? Is it too technical? Does it need special skills and knowledge to go through the journey? Do you need to be lucky to get through to the end of this journey? Do you need any specialized financial degrees? You will realize while reading this book that the answer to all these questions is a resounding "No". All these things may give you an edge at some stage of this journey but they are not mandatory and neither do they guarantee successful completion of the journey. Then what is it that makes 99% unsuccessful and only 1% successful in this journey of financial freedom? As with most great things in life, the answer is a set of very simple steps and changes in some habits that we all need to bring about in ourselves to break this deadly trap. Was it easy? No. It is never easy to change yourself and my case was no different. Was it worth it? Absolutely, it was.

It took me 7 years from the day I initiated a financial freedom[1] plan to reach even close to financial freedom but each learning, every change, every sacrifice was worth its weight in gold. It is definitely worth it today as I know that I am not dependent on anyone to take care of my family. It is worth it as I know that true happiness comes from "giving" and not "taking" from others and I am capable of "giving" now. It is worth it as I can now spend time and money on fulfilling the "real" goals of my life and spend time doing what I love doing rather than what gives me more money. Each and every moment now is worth living.

This book will lead you through a step by step journey on how I achieved it. It will also tell you under what circumstances I took some specific financial decisions so that you can map them with their circumstances and take a decision that is more appropriate for you. Anyone even an absolute novice without any knowledge about financial planning and financial freedom can benefit from my example, since I started from Ground Zero.

The financial planning exercises in the book starts with some fundamental definitions and terms one must know. It uses illustrative examples to explain those definitions. Once a basic understanding of the financial terms is developed, the book will walk you through all the financial investment options available today in the Indian market with the relative merits and demerits of all such options. All views expressed are based on my personal experience and hence are illustrated with actual examples. I do not expect you to start investing just by reading these examples and using these investment tools. This book is intended to bring your financial literacy to the fore besides setting the right perspective for you to get a broader view of things.

Once the technicalities are clear, the book goes on to deal with the most critical, and often the most neglected, parts of such a journey. I realized that this is where 99% of the people fail. This part of the book is about the habitual changes that we all need to bring in ourselves if we have to successfully complete this journey. The book lists all healthy habits that I had to inculcate in myself and how I did that. Success principles do not change. You may have heard or read about many of these habits, but the key is how to implement them in one's own life.

Once you have the technical expertise and know what habitual changes are needed to be successful, the much awaited section of the book opens up. This is something I never found in any book I read during my journey to financial freedom. It deals with my entire financial planning, based on my income and expenses today and my present assets and liabilities. How do I actually plan my own journey step by step? How do I make month on month goals? What goals are right for me? How do I document them? Once I have documented them, how can I track them month on month to make sure that I am staying on track till I reach financial freedom? What kind of tracking mechanisms can be adopted to make sure that my freedom nest stays healthy?

I often compare financial freedom with a nation's freedom. Why is it so important for a country to be free? Perhaps because a country wants to take certain decisions which it feels are in its best interest under the given circumstances for its future. It wants to take those decisions and wants to be free to be able to take those decisions. Similarly, it is a fundamental trait of human beings that they want to be able to take their own decisions in life and then apply them and experience the results. The reader can take those decisions if he or she is out of the rat race and enjoys what is popularly known as "financial freedom". This is the reader's personal freedom, which is no less important than a nation's freedom.

The good news is that this freedom is not that difficult to achieve and the best news is that it is all in your hands. The book gives you a direction and illustrates how a common man like me has done it. The ball is in your court now!!

Go for it.....

Overview

Even if you win the Rat Race, you are still a Rat.
— **Lily Tomlin**

Wikipedia defines a rat race as follows:

"Rat race is a term used for an endless, self-defeating or pointless pursuit. It conjures up the image of the futile efforts of a lab rat trying to escape while running around a maze or in a wheel. In an analogy to the modern city, many rats in a single maze expend a lot of effort running around, but ultimately achieve nothing (meaningful) either collectively or individually."

How many of us can relate to this? Well, I was able to relate fully. I am sure many more like me can relate to this continuous running and achieving nothing meaningful in the end.

You are well paid, well off and have a good lifestyle. But can you afford to stop working? If your answer is 'No', then you are just financially stable[7] and far from being financially independent or financially free.

Believe me, you are not the only one. Most people – more than 99% of the working class retire without being financially independent. They are in a vicious cycle – the rat race as it is commonly called. They never have enough money to retire. Even after retirement, they are struggling to make ends meet and are seen to be in need of some kind of work to continue to survive. What kind of life is this where we are so engrossed in our own survival that we cannot even think about bringing about any change in our society or doing something for anyone other than our own family?

This is exactly what I was going through, when I realized that there has to be a way out of this mindless and meaningless rat race. As you will see all through in this book, there is immense power in what we will refer to as the super power of compounded money.

However, this book is not about retiring and leading a lonely life, neither is it about quitting challenges in life. This book is about achieving the most important personal freedom that every human being is looking for — your own financial freedom. Why is this important? Because the absence of financial freedom is the only thing which keeps us from achieving the best in life and from doing what we most enjoy.

What do you really want to do with the time and money that you have?

Do you still want to go and work in a stressful job? Do you want to continue in the rat race and keep working for your money? Do you want to struggle for the next salary increment or promotion? Do you want to keep blaming your luck, government laws and the world for the fact that your business is not able to survive anymore? Does your family have to always take second priority because your boss or your business takes first priority? Do you still want to say that "You have no choice"? Do you still want to keep hating Mondays? Do you want to always be looking for a new job because you are not "satisfied" in your current job? Do you still want to feel victimized and continue to lead an unhappy life?

Or do you want to wake up every morning and decide what challenges you will overcome today? Do you want to drop your children to school because you have the freedom of time? Would you rather be with your family and friends at celebratory occasions, than be compelled to attend a client meeting? Do you want to be able to give a gift to friends and family on their birthdays, anniversaries, and other smaller milestones in their lives without thinking of the financial impact on you? Do you want to serve society and/or help your nation? Do you want the freedom to decide what you want to do? Do you want to do what you really enjoy rather than be compelled to earn more money?

If the answer to any of the above questions is "Yes", then you have the right book in your hand. That's what this book is all about. It's all about your freedom to decide and choose what you want to do every day in your life. Imagine a life where "you and only you" have the freedom to decide what you want to do today. Believe me it is possible!

The good news is that each one of us can be financially

independent, irrespective of our present income level. We can all become independent of the monthly pay cheques that we are so heavily dependent upon. We just need to take very simple basic steps, plan a little better and make more disciplined savings and investments. Subsequent chapters in this book will give you a step by step guide on how this can be achieved. This is not theoretical. I have done it myself. Coming from a middle class background and having a so called good income, it took me almost 13 years of being in a good, high profile job to realize the importance of financial independence[3] over a high profile job.

The choice was always with me. That no one guided me was always an excuse. I never thought that there could be a life without a job or without having to work and earn money. This misconception was mainly because of what I saw all around me – my parents, my family, my colleagues, my friends. I had never heard anyone using terms like financial freedom, independence or wealth creation. Even if someone used these terms, they never believed that they themselves could ever be financially free.

I want to assure you that this freedom is possible. It is possible to shape your life the way you want it. If you are facing a crisis today, only you are responsible for it, no one else, and only you can resolve it. God has given everyone equal capability and time to do whatever they want to do with their lives.

Now, it is up to you to decide what you want to do. You can spend your entire life in pursuit of money or become financially free and use money as a means of achieving your ultimate goals.

It is Possible!

1

Wealth Myths

*There are two kinds of money problems in this world... one-
you have a lot of money and the other — you have no money.
You choose which problem you want!!*

*— **Anonymous***

Wealth is the slave of a wise man and the master of a fool!!
*— **Seneca***

*I can understand wanting to have a million dollars
— it's freedom.*
*— **Bill Gates***

Who becomes wealthy?

I always believed myself to be financially unlucky to have been born in a middle class family where all of us had to struggle all our lives to first make our ends meet and then support our family's needs. By the time, we could understand money and financials we were already in a trap which was almost impossible to break. It is referred to as the "rat race" in the previous section. You have a family to support and you can never save enough to earn a passive income. The pool of money never grows big enough to self sustain inflation and all the expenses that we must incur as a part of our life responsibilities.

It was while reading one of the books on becoming a millionaire[2] that I realized that 80% of America's millionaires are first generation ones. They did it slowly, steadily and without signing any multimillion dollar deals. Read it again — 80% of the millionaires are self made and are first generation. This fact just cut through the whole "excuse wall" that I had built up around myself.

What this fact essentially meant was that it is not the inherited money that counts; it is the effort and discipline that you put in during your lifetime that makes you rich. So, if you thought you can never be a millionaire, think again.

I went on to read many such books on how people became millionaires and found the following common traits in first generation millionaires:

1. They live well below their means.

2. They allocate their time, energy, and money efficiently, in ways conducive to wealth building.

3. They strongly believe and live the fact that financial independence is more important than displaying high social status.

4. Their parents were not financially well off or even if they were, they did not provide economic support.

5. Their adult children are economically self sufficient.

6. They married once and remained married.

7. They did not fail "because of ..." but succeeded "in spite of...". Failure was never an option for them.

8. They live next door to people with a small fraction of their wealth (The major portion of their wealth is wisely invested).

9. They are compulsive savers and investors of money...all of which they have made on their own.

10. They have confidence in their own abilities.

There can be many other traits but if you look at the above ten traits of self made, fist generation millionaires, what does it tell you? One thing that it clearly tells you is that it is possible for anyone to do it. Of course, you need to plan it out and then execute the plan, but it is not outside your reach. Imagine the quality of life that you could enjoy if you were financially free.

I just want to reproduce some lines here from one of the most fundamental yet most powerful and famous books ever written on the principles of wealth accumulation: *The Richest Man in Babylon*.

▶ Money is the medium by which earthly success is measured.

▶ Money makes possible the enjoyment of the best the earth affords.

▶ Money is plentiful for those who understand the simple laws which govern its acquisition.

- Money is governed today by the same laws which controlled it when prosperous men thronged the streets of Babylon, six thousand years ago.

Once you have understood these simple, yet powerful laws – money will not stay too far away from you.

And I can assure you that once you have "enough" money, you will find enough ways to utilize it the way it is supposed to be utilized. The world looks completely different with enough money in your hands.

What would be your confidence level in your office or in dealing with a client on Monday morning if you realized that you are not dependent on the monthly pay check that the company gives you? The difference would be astonishing. There would be a sense of self confidence and a fearless approach to things.

Life can surely be much more beautiful with enough money in your hands.

Why do I need wealth?

Some of you may have a valid question that may occur to you time and again. It obviously strikes you more as you become more mature with age and experience.

Is life about money?

No, life is not about money. It is about God. It is about love, family and relationships. It is about "giving" instead of "taking" or "becoming". It is also about personal evolution and growth across all spheres of life – physical, mental and spiritual. And anyone who tells you otherwise is probably trying to sell you something.

I cannot think of any method certain of creating an unhappy life than to devote it to the primary pursuit of money.

However, the pursuit of financial freedom to secure and enhance life's true needs is not only perfectly appropriate but also wise. For those, who do not accept the responsibility of financial freedom at an early age, get thrown out of balance at a later stage in life.

As the Bible says,
"Money is not the root of evils". It is the "love for money" that is the root of all evils.

Money is just an instrument. It is up to us what we want to do with this powerful instrument. What is more important is not to get attached to money. Use it. Use it to take care of you and your family. Use it for others' benefit. Use it to help others. Accumulate more and use more to educate under privileged children. Use it the way it is supposed to be used and it will never cause any evil.

It is in fact the lack of money that is the root of all evil. Financial distress is an evil. 90% of all divorces have a common cause of quarrels traced back to money and finances. Debt and poverty lead to other serious social evils.

What can you give to others if you are yourself stuck in a stressful, seven days a week, job or are struggling to meet your own family's daily needs? What physical health can you guarantee for yourself and your family with all the stress and physical pain of going through and doing something which does not make you happy?

It reminds me of a very common instruction we hear whilst boarding a aircraft — in case of an emergency during the flight, oxygen masks will descend from above your seat, please make sure that you put on your mask before helping your children or neighbour with their mask. Why do they say this? Is it not selfish? No, it is just wise. If you cannot breathe properly how will you be able to help anyone else?

It is exactly the same with accumulating wealth and getting rich. It is a pre-requisite to helping others.

Financial freedom through wealth accumulation gives you all the freedom to do what you really want to do in life.

 **So, what's the POINT?** You need money to use it the way that it is intended to be used.

Do you need to invest?

Before we understand the term 'financial freedom', we must understand the term investment[8] and the reasons why we should invest at all. You have your money in the bank and the bank is anyway paying you a "decent" interest besides keeping your money safe. So, do you think you really need to invest your money elsewhere?

Yes, you do.

If your money cannot beat the running inflation after paying all taxes, it is actually going down in value every month and every year. Since the money lying in your fixed deposits will never be able to achieve this you have got to "invest".

Investment is all about beating inflation and taxes

There are primarily 3 categories in which you can invest your money —

- ▸ Cash investments like saving accounts

- ▸ Income investments like FDs, bonds

- ▸ Growth investments like equities, art and real estate

Inflation

Sam Ewing, a humorist, defines inflation very beautifully:

> *Inflation is when you pay 15 $ for the 10 $ haircut you used to get for 5 $ when you had hair.*

So, in a nutshell, if you leave all your money in the savings account, you are losing money every day. Inflation is a reality in day to day life. You will read more about why inflation occurs in the subsequent sections of the book. But let me try to give you a layman's example of what happens to your money because of inflation.

Let us say that you have ₹ 1000/- in your savings account today and the current inflation rate is 8%. If you continue to keep the money in a traditional bank savings account, it earns you an interest of approx 4%. In effect, at the end of Year 1, your money would have grown to ₹ 1040/-. Though we may see this as growth, the sad part is that Inflation eats into all this growth. After Year 1, your money is worth 8% less which means it is now actually worth ₹ 957/- (if you compare it with the same parameters as ₹ 1000/- at Year 0).

Even at the low rate of 3% per annum, inflation eats up a quarter of your money's purchasing power every 10 years. In 24 years, your money is reduced to half. That is a fairly large number and that too at a very conservative rate of 3%. Watch what happens when this number begins to climb. At 5%, your purchasing power is reduced to half in mere 14 years and at 6%, it just takes 12 years for inflation to do the same damage.

At the time of writing this book, the inflation rate in India is almost touching double digits. So most of us cannot even imagine the speed at which the value of money is eroding. Whenever we hear about price increases and the difficulty of meeting our needs because of high prices, it is nothing but inflation that is unknowingly being referred to. If you do nothing with the wealth that you have accumulated, it will just erode with time.

You have no choice. You have to "invest".

The equity market[6] (and also investment in precious metals like gold) presents the best guard against inflation. Bank fixed deposits and other investment tools would at most keep up with inflation, but over time, good companies normally stay ahead of inflation. The equity market offers the best potential for long-term growth. You may still experience certain unsettling downs, but with patience, you will always stay ahead. You should never aim at making money overnight in the equity market.

So, fundamentally, there is something wrong going around which needs your intervention to stay on track, and that 'intervention' is the investment you make across the spectrum of tools available and described in detail in this book. The investment has to be made in such a way that your money is safe and secure and also gives you a rate of return which can beat the rate of inflation.

So, what's the **POINT** If you do not invest and fortify your portfolio against inflation, you will surely outlive your money.

What it takes to be a wise investor

Now you know that you need to invest your money, you must also know how and where to invest it wisely so that it not only gives you enough returns to beat inflation but also assures that your basic invested amount is safe and secure.

Let us try and find out what it takes to be a wise investor.

What do you think it takes to be a wise investor?

- An MBA degree

- A sixth sense about timing in the market?

- Years of spending 60 hours a week on Dalal Street or Wall Street

- Talent – a certain ability that certain people are just born with

- Luck

Well, the answer is none of the above.

Anyone, and everyone, can become a wise investor.

To do so, you need to do only two fundamental things:

1. Learn the basics of investing then

2. Execute the basics and stick to them.

Once you learn the basics, you will always be able to handle the financial part of your life and the reason for that is very simple. The reason is that the economy changes, our needs and goals change, the market changes, but the basic strategies always remain the same. You have to just learn them once.

Investing is a lifelong commitment. Investing is not a game. It is about the things that matter most to you.

2

Technical Concepts in
Financial Independence

The rich invest their money and spend what is left;
the poor spend their money and invest what is left.
— Jim Rohn

In the simplest technical definitions, if your assets[9] are more than your liabilities[10] and your net worth[11] (assets minus liabilities) is greater than or equal to the expenditure needed to maintain your standard of living, then you can be said to be financially independent.

An asset is anything that pays you.

A liability is anything that you pay for.

Financial independence is also defined as a state where you are free from all liabilities and have created sufficient wealth that can generate a constant stream of income that allows you to maintain your lifestyle without having to work for it. Remember that the wealth pool should be big enough to take care of inflation (after taxes) as well as your monthly expenses for the rest of your life.

How much can be considered sufficient? What should your net worth be for your age group and for your standard of living so that you can be termed as financially independent or wealthy?

Well, there is no readymade formula which gives you a definite number. But normally, financial planners use a very simple technique to determine whether you are saving enough or not, depending on your age group and level of income

If your net worth is at least equal to your Annual income* Age/10, then you can be termed as wealthy, otherwise not. The same formula is expressed in the table on the following page for different age groups and income levels for ease of reference. I would like to re-emphasize that there is neither a magical formula nor a rule of thumb to define wealthy people. The table on the following page is just a guideline to see where you stand as on date with respect to the so called global standards of wealthy people.

For example, from the table below, you should save enough to have a net worth of approximately ₹ 72 lacs, if your age is in the range of 31 to 35 years and your present annual income is in the range of ₹ 15 to 20 lacs.

Table of net worth (₹ lacs) with age (years) and annual income (₹ lacs)

Age/ Annual income (₹ lacs)	<5L	5-10L	10-15L	15-20L	21-30L	31-40L	41-50L	> 50L
20 – 25	10L	20L	30L	40L	60L	80L	100L	>150L
26 – 30	14L	28L	42L	56L	84L	112L	140L	>225L
31 – 35	18L	36L	54L	72L	108L	145L	180L	>300L
36 – 40	22L	44L	66L	88L	130L	175L	220L	>350L
41 – 45	25L	50L	75L	100L	150L	200L	250L	>400L
45 – 50	30L	60L	90L	120L	180L	240L	300L	>450L
51 – 60	35L	70L	105L	140L	210L	280L	350L	>525L

Apart from all the standard financial and technical definitions, I would like to define financial independence as the "freedom" to choose what you really want to do with your life, and that is why I prefer to call it "financial freedom", rather than anything else. Most of us have been living as slaves to money for most of our lives and have absolutely no idea as to how important the idea of financial freedom can be.

Most people I have met during my professional career, have either never imagined what can be achieved with this financial freedom or even if they had that imagination, they never knew how to get out of the rat race in which they are stuck. Each of them had a reason to continue in that race and they all felt they were victims of their circumstances.

If you have ever had this feeling, you need not ever feel that way again. You have everything that is needed to come out of this mess. Just follow what I am about to tell you, step by step.

We will start by understanding certain concepts which will form the basis for you to take the fundamental investment decisions, given later in the book. You should read them as many times as you need and be comfortable with these concepts. It is not reasonable to expect that you would understand everything during the first reading.

This book deals with very simple fundamental concepts for beginners on this journey. I have tried my level best to give you only the bare minimum financial concepts which are essential for you to take investment decisions later on. In case you have any difficulty in understanding any of the financial concepts, please feel free to drop an email at help@ratrace2freedom.com.

There is a treasure of information to share with all of you who are passionate about your financial freedom. This includes templates and formats for your financial planning, information and views from around the globe from people who are passionately pursuing the financial freedom goals; and the latest experiences I have gone through that can help you reach the goals faster and also build a strong investment portfolio. I have collated all this and you can avail it at the following website — www.ratrace2freedom.com. Please feel free to register, login and access all this invaluable information. This website is about, and for everyone who wants to experience the pleasure of financial freedom or those that are already experiencing it.

It contains detailed examples of these fundamental concepts and gives you a chance to try out examples with your own financial situations.

This book, website, helpdesk and all other tools are at your disposal. If at any stage, you are still not satisfied, please do not hesitate to contact me directly.

I sincerely want you to be financially free so that you can get the time to contribute in your own way to make this world a better place to live in.

Let us now go ahead with learning some essential financial concepts. Some of these concepts may seem very simple for some of you but keeping the general reader in mind, it was important for me to present these concepts at this stage. This book is especially focused on the reader who has long-term plans for financial freedom. Even if you are comfortable with any specific topic, it is still recommended that you go through them to get the right perspective of money and investments as we proceed further in the book.

Knowledge of these fundamental concepts not only helps us to invest wisely the first time, but also allows us to correctly track the returns coming from the invested amount so that we can tune our investment decisions accordingly.

Let us start with a brief history of money and learning about the basic fundamentals of money. Thereafter, we will follow the topics listed in the table below.

Technical Concepts in Financial Independence	
Evolution of Money	Cost Inflation Index
Absolute Returns	Taxes
Annualized Simple Interest Returns	Capital Gain (Loss) Tax
Compounded Annual Growth Rate (CAGR)	Dollar Cost Averaging
Internal Rate of Return (IRR)	Rule of 72
	Portfolio Asset Allocation

Technical Concepts in Financial Independence	
Evolution of Money	Cost Inflation Index
Absolute Returns	Taxes
Annualized Simple Interest Returns	Capital Gain (Loss) Tax
Compounded Annual Growth Rate (CAGR)	Dollar Cost Averaging
Internal Rate of Return (IRR)	Rule of 72
	Portfolio Asset Allocation

Evolution of Money

Money evolved as human society grew more sophisticated and required a more convenient way to transact business. As Robert Kiyosaki terms it, you would see that "real money" has now got transformed to "magic or funny money".

Barter

We have all studied the barter system[12] in our history books at some stage of our schooling. It is important to go through this again and see how these finally lead to the creation of money in its current form.

The barter system was original form of doing business, in which one could trade one product or service for another. While this is "the real" business, the obvious problem with this system was that it was extremely slow, tedious and time consuming. On the positive side, it was hard for the government to tax any barter trade. As the economy goes through recession, you might see some barter still happening and even increasing in today's world.

Commodities

To overcome the sluggishness in the barter system and to speed up the way people traded, people agreed on tangible items as "representative" value. For example, seashells, goats, gold, silver etc., became commodities and represented some value which could help people barter more efficiently.

Let me explain the need of commodities through a very simple example. Let us take a real business situation where person A wants to buy a plot of land and person B (who has a plot of land to sell) wants to buy a tractor. How could they barter using the barter trading system if A does not have tractor? They cannot. But commodities[13] make this possible.

If A had the commodities which represent some unit of value, this trade becomes possible even if A does not have a tractor. Let us say, A had some standardized gold coins, then he/she could buy the piece of land and give equivalent gold coins worth the price of the land to the seller (Person B). Person B can then take those gold coins and look for a person C (anyone who wants to sell a tractor). Person C need not be interested in buying land but only in selling a tractor. So, whatever trade was not feasible in the barter system between Person A and Person B became feasible in a commodity[13] based system between Persons A, B and C.

That is how the use of commodities hastened the process of exchange and more business could be done in less time. Even today, gold and silver are internationally accepted commodities as money. In fact, they are considered more valuable than paper money. While paper money is "national", gold and silver were always "international" commodities.

Receipt money

As business grew, commodities became more important and more prevalent. "Rich" people would have more commodities than the not so rich ones. As the gap between the "rich" and "poor" grew, the safety of commodities became more and more important.

To keep precious metals and gems (like gold, silver, diamonds etc.,) safe, wealthy people put their gold and other commodities in "safe hands" and in turn received a receipt. This was the start of banking. Remember that the receipt money (or paper money as we know it today) was just a derivative[14] and no more a tangible item like gold. As money evolved from a tangible item of value to a derivative of value i.e., a receipt, the speed of business definitely increased. Whenever traders used to travel over long distances, they used to carry receipts of the commodities they owned rather than the commodities themselves (due to the fear of theft) and would also pay as receipts.

Modern day banking starts here. The seller would take the receipt from the buyer and deposit it in the bank. Rather than transfer the commodities from one location to another with each such transaction, the two bankers in the two cities would reconcile the trading accounts between the buyer and seller with debits and credits against receipts. This further increased the speed of business. Some of the modern forms of receipt money are cheques, bank drafts etc.

For example, a modern day cheque is like a receipt issued by the safe keeper of your commodities (bank) which you can fill in with an amount less than or equal to the commodities held by the bank and the bank will honour your receipt to the seller whenever the receipt is presented to the bank.

Even a currency note is a receipt. If you read carefully what is written on a currency note, you will find that the currency note says that the bank promises to pay the possessor of the currency note an amount equivalent to the rupees stated in that currency note. The note actually has no value of its own. It is just a receipt from the bank promising to pay that amount worth of commodities.

While cheque books are the kind of receipts where the value can be entered manually depending on what the consumer purchases, currency notes are receipts issued by the banks and promise to pay a fixed amount to the bearer of that currency note. As long as you trust this bank, you can continue to hold this currency note and trade other items for it.

When there is a trust deficit on the bank, you will see people going back to "actual commodities" like gold and silver rather than these currency notes and other form of receipts.

Fractional reserve receipt money

As wealth increased through trade, banks became full of precious commodities such as gold, silver and gems. Bankers realized that customers had no use for these precious commodities and were comfortable trading with receipts.

Banks got greedier. To make more money, banks moved from "storing wealth" to "lending wealth," which means they started issuing money or receipts without any backing of commodities with them.

What it essentially meant was that they were now printing money. Since the central banks were making money from the interest received on the receipts they issued like currency notes (and not the actual commodities they held), they wanted to issue more and more receipts. More notes were being printed without any commodity backup, ultimately resulting in Inflation.

So, in any country, the central bank could issue more and more currency notes and start earning from the interest received from those currency notes even if there was no backing for those receipts or currency notes by equivalent commodities. So the biggest change here was that while the commodities were limited, there was virtually no limit to the number and amount of receipts that could be issued.

There was obviously a flip side to this entire expansion and greed, which is commonly called inflation[15].

Inflation arose with the increase in costs. Inflation started going up for the first time as notes were being printed without any commodity backup. For ₹ 1000/- worth of commodities with the bank, the bank started issuing receipts (and hence started earning interest) for say, ₹ 2000/- (a fractional reserve[90] of 2:1).

As greed grew, cases came to light in which banks started going bankrupt when they issued more money than the commodities they held and got withdrawal requests which they could not honour.

This is one of the most important reasons why central banks[16] like the Federal Reserve Bank in the US and the Reserve Bank of India were created. These banks, not only wanted only one form of money — currency or commodity, but they also needed to regulate the fractional reserve system so that it did not go out of control.

Fiat money

Until now, things were still somewhat in control as long as the central government banks were controlling the fractional reserve ratio. However, as we all know, greed knows no end.

In 1971, the US Dollar was severed from the gold standard. Therefore, the US no longer needed any commodities to create money. Technically, prior to 1971, the US Dollar was a derivative of gold but post 1971 the US Dollar became a derivative of debt.

"Fiat" literally means an authoritative order. Fiat money is money which is not backed even by a fractional commodity. It is just issued on the government's faith and trust backing. It is more authoritative rather than being logical.

Coins

Coins, as you see them today, were derived from gold and silver commodities. Since gold and silver were precious and were always prone to threats, there was a need to replace them with something that cannot be stolen so easily.

In the early stages of the life history of coins, they were made of gold and silver and represented a certain unit of gold or silver. As it happened with money receipts, the banks and the governments across the globe started mixing these precious metals with certain base metals like aluminium and copper to ease business and reduce theft risk.

Today the coins are anything but gold or silver.

This is essentially how money originated.

Having now gone through the background and history of barter, commodities, money and coins, let us come to the present day and look at some of the financial terms, definitions and formulas, which is critical for us to understand before we start looking at any kind of investments.

Let us start with the meaning of "returns[17]" and how we can calculate them.

Technical Concepts in Financial Independence	
Evolution of Money	Cost Inflation Index
Absolute Returns	Taxes
Annualized Simple Interest Returns	Capital Gain (Loss) Tax
Compounded Annual Growth Rate (CAGR)	Dollar Cost Averaging
Internal Rate of Return (IRR)	Rule of 72
	Portfolio Asset Allocation

Absolute Returns

Now that you are aware of the history of money and how it originated, we are in a better shape to discuss how some of the fundamental calculations actually work for modern day money investments.

One of the most critical aspects to be measured on the investments you make is the Return On Investments[17] (ROI). As stated previously, you have no choice but to invest your money so that you can beat inflation and taxes, which means that your money should actually grow on investing it.

To find out whether that is happening or not, or to find the rate at which your money is growing vis-a-vis the inflation rate and taxes, there are certain prescribed methods to calculate the returns from your investments.

The most common method that people use to calculate the return on their investment is absolute returns[18]

Let us take a very simple example to illustrate the concept of absolute returns. Remember that absolute returns are "absolute" by definition. This means that these returns are calculated without taking any time period into account.

As you go through the examples overleaf, do not bother about the terms used in the example like NAV or NFO etc. These terms are not important at this stage. You will get a detailed understanding of these terms as you go through the rest of the book. The focus right now is just to understand how the return on investments can be calculated

Formula 1

Absolute ROI= $\dfrac{\text{(Current Market Value} - \text{Cost of Investment)}}{\text{(Cost of Investment)}}$

Example 1

I invested in equity New Fund Offer (NFO) two years back at ₹ 10 per unit (assuming no entry load). Today the Net Asset Value (NAV) quoted for that mutual fund stands at ₹ 15 per unit. What is the return on my invested amount?

Solution: Calculating Absolute ROI

The absolute return calculation based on Formula 1 would come out to be:

Absloute ROI   = (15-10)/10
                = 5/10
                = 0.5 (or 50%)

So, the case of Example 1 would give 50% Absolute ROI in our case.

While this kind of returns is easy to calculate, they do not account for the time period in which the returns have been achieved. As you can see that 50% returns in the above example was a result of 2 years of investment. The time period for returns is a very important factor because the money that may have eroded because of inflation depends on the time period.

Also, it becomes almost impossible to see which investment is better than the other if these investments are done over different time periods.

Let us go to the next step and look at a little more advanced way of calculating returns, which also account for the time period in which returns have been received.

Technical Concepts in Financial Independence	
Evolution of Money	Cost Inflation Index
Absolute Returns	Taxes
Annualized Simple Interest Returns	Capital Gain (Loss) Tax
Compounded Annual Growth Rate (CAGR)	Dollar Cost Averaging
Internal Rate of Return (IRR)	Rule of 72
	Portfolio Asset Allocation

Annualized Simple Interest Returns

Now that you know that absolute returns may not be the best way to compare returns received from different investment tools across different time periods, we can use another simple formula which can help us provide an annualized version of the returns on investment. We term this as Simple Annual ROI[19].

Formula 2

$$\text{Simple Annual ROI} = \frac{(\text{Current Market Value} - \text{Cost of Investment})}{(\text{Cost of Investment})}$$

Let us use a modification of Example 1 to illustrate the concept of annualized simple interest rate returns.

Example 2

I invested in equity NFO two years back at ₹ 10 per unit (assuming no entry load). Today the NAV quoted for that mutual fund stands at ₹ 15 per unit. What is the annualized return on my invested amount?

Solution 2: Calculating Annualized Simple ROI

The annualized simple return calculation is based on Formula 2. It is:

Annualized Simple ROI = (15-10)/(10*2)

= 5/20

= 0.25 (or 25%)

So, the case of Example 2 would give 25% annualized simple ROI in our case.

This is definitely simple, and yet a more realistic and comparative method of calculation for returns on a year to year basis.

Now, I am in a position to compare two different investments made over different periods of time. However, there are some limitations here as well.

Do note that the formula for Simple Annual ROI works only if you have invested once at the beginning of a multi-year tenure and get the returns also once at the end of the tenure. This method of calculating returns becomes invalid if there are investments or returns in the middle of this tenure.

This formula will get further tuned as we consider a multi-year spread of investments as well as returns in a later part of the book.

Before that however, there is one very critical element in returns calculation that needs to be introduced at this stage, namely interest[20]. In all practical scenarios, we need to consider the fact that the interest earned each year in a multi-year tenure is re-invested for the next year and also contributes to the return in the next year.

This method of calculation where the interest earned is re-invested for the future tenure and contributes to the overall returns is called as Compounded Annual Growth Rate[21] (CAGR).

Let us now look at an example of how to calculate CAGR for a multi-year investment where the interest is re-invested as a principal[22] for the next year's returns.

Technical Concepts in Financial Independence	
Evolution of Money	Cost Inflation Index
Absolute Returns	Taxes
Annualized Simple Interest Returns	Capital Gain (Loss) Tax
Compounded Annual Growth Rate (CAGR)	Dollar Cost Averaging
Internal Rate of Return (IRR)	Rule of 72
	Portfolio Asset Allocation

Compounded Annual Growth Rate (CAGR)

The Compounded Annual Growth Rate, as the name suggests, takes care of two critical factors to give a true picture of the returns on your investment viz "compounded" and "annual." It assumes that the gains are re-invested every year and these re-invested gains further contribute to the overall returns.

Remember that this formula still assumes that the investments are made once at the beginning of the multi-year tenure and returns are received once at the end of the multi-year tenure. The interest earned out of the investment, however, is re-invested and contributes to the overall returns.

Calculating CAGR

The CAGR is calculated using Formula 3:

Formula 3

CAGR= [(Current market Value) / (Cost of Investment) $]^{(1/n)}$ – 1

Where 'n' is the number of years for which the amount was invested
Let us use a modification of Example 2 to illustrate the concept of CAGR and how it is different from simple annualized returns.

Example 3

I invested in equity NFO two years back at ₹ 10 per unit (assuming no entry load). Today the NAV quoted for that mutual fund stands at ₹ 15 per unit. What is the annualized return on my invested amount if I were to assume that any interest earned in the first year is re-invested back in the second year?

Solution 3: Calculating Annualized Simple ROI

The CAGR calculation is based on Formula 3. The calculation would be as follows:

CAGR
$$= (15/10)^{(1/2)} - 1$$
$$= 1.5^{0.5} - 1$$
$$= 1.225 - 1$$
$$= 0.225 \text{ (or } 22.5\%)$$

So, the calculations based on Example 3 would give 22.5% CAGR returns in our case.

This method of compounded return calculation is more realistic and represents how the money "actually" grows in your saving banks or fixed deposits that give a definite interest rate for a defined period, assuming that you have not opted for interest pay out option. The interest pay out option essentially means that the annual return is paid out to you separately and the money does not grow in a compounded manner.

Note that in comparison to Example 2, which used simple rate of interest, you could get the same returns in Example 3 using a lesser rate of interest or rate of return (22.5% with CAGR as against 25% with Simple ROI). This goes to prove the importance of compounded interest. It also proves the fact that if the rate of interest is the same for Simple ROI and CAGR, then CAGR gives you higher returns.

The CAGR formula is the one which can help you calculate the immense power of compounding over a period of time. We will see the power of compounding in more detail later in the book.

However, there is still a limitation with this formula, it assumes that you invest the money once and then let it grow in a compounded manner and get all the returns on a definite date. With traditional investment tools like savings accounts and fixed deposits, this formula works fairly accurately because these two types of investment work within the constraints of a definite amount invested for a definite period.

However, for your investments to really give you returns that beat inflation, we need to diversify our investments to other investment tools. If that is the case, then how do we calculate the returns for investments like mutual funds, stocks and other investments, which take periodic as well as irregularly sized investments over irregular periods of times? Over and above this, part of the investments may mature during the defined time period. Actually, there is no defined time period or amount to invest or for returns in such cases. Understandably, these calculations can get really complex and it is difficult to obtain accurate results through a simple mathematical formula.

As complex as it can get, the best way to do return calculations in such complex scenarios is through a method that we call the Internal Rate of Return[23] (IRR), as explained in the next section.

Technical Concepts in Financial Independence	
Evolution of Money	Cost Inflation Index
Absolute Returns	Taxes
Annualized Simple Interest Returns	Capital Gain (Loss) Tax
Compounded Annual Growth Rate (CAGR)	Dollar Cost Averaging
Internal Rate of Return (IRR)	Rule of 72
	Portfolio Asset Allocation

Internal Rate of Return (IRR)

The Internal Rate of Return (IRR) is a rate of return used in capital budgeting to measure and compare the profitability of investments. It is also called the Discounted Cash Flow Rate of Return (DCFROR[23]) or simply the Rate of Return (ROR). In the context of savings and loans, the IRR is also called the effective interest rate. The term "internal" refers to the fact that its calculation does not incorporate environmental factors (e.g., the interest rate or inflation) but incorporates the time factor of multiple investments.

Generally, calculation of IRR is very cumbersome and we cannot use many theoretical formulae to calculate this. Most of us make use of Microsoft Excel's standard formula of IRR to calculate it.

Calculating IRR

The ground rules for calculating IRR are as follows:

1. All investments must be captured with a negative sign (indicating outflow of money).

2. All returns must be captured with a positive sign (indicating inflow of money).

3. A table of investments and returns must be created in chronological order over time.

4. The periods used when creating a table of investment and returns must be standard i.e., either use weeks or months or years but do not use a combination of any of these periods in the same table.

5. The IRR formula will give you the returns for the period used in the table i.e., if you have used months as the standard period for a particular table, the IRR formula will give you the returns per month.

Given below is an example of how IRR is actually calculated.

Are you getting confused or lost? If yes, don't worry. Do not hurry up either. Do not skip this section without understanding it completely. Read it again and then follow the example below to understand it. It is important for you to understand it, if you wish to become a millionaire. It is worth spending time and energy to prepare yourself for perhaps the most critical journey of your life.

You will need to use this almost on an everyday basis as you start dealing with more and more money and start comparing your returns from across multiple investments.

Once you are thoroughly familiar with the concept, move forward and have a look at the example to see how we can calculate the IRR for Systematic Investment Plan[24] (SIP) based mutual funds investments done yearly over a period of a few years and the returns in a specific year.

Example 4

I invested varied amounts in Reliance mutual funds starting from 2007 till 2010 as per the following details: ₹ 6,000 in 2007, ₹ 20,000 in 2008, ₹ 30,000 in 2009 and ₹ 12,000 in 2010. The NAV of the invested amount as on 31st Dec 2010 is ₹. 101,800. On the other hand, I am getting a 15% rate of return in UTI mutual funds. I need to make a decision for investments in the coming year, 2011.

Should I continue to invest in Reliance mutual funds in 2011 or should I switch to UTI mutual funds?

Solution 4: Calculating IRR

For all such complex scenarios where you have a varied kind of investments and withdrawals over multiple periods of time, we will use the IRR method to calculate the IRR for Reliance mutual funds at the end of 2010 and then compare it with the rate of return from UTI mutual funds to make a decision for 2011.

Step 1

Open up a Microsoft Excel spreadsheet and enter the annual investments in one column with a negative sign (indicating outflow of money), as shown in Figure 1.

Mutual Funds	
Investment	
Year	Amount
2007	-6,000
2008	-20,000
2009	-30,000
2010	-12,000

Fig 1: *Step 1 for Solution 4*

Step 2

Assume that you will sell off the entire mutual fund portfolio today. Enter the current value of the total invested amount to date in the last cell in the same column with a positive value (indicating inflow).

Mutual Funds	
Investment	
Year	Amount
2007	-6,000
2008	-20,000
2009	-30,000
2010	-12,000
2011	
Value as on Dec 2010	1,01,800

Fig 2: *Step 2 for Solution 4*

Step 3

Use the Excel IRR formula in the last row to calculate the annualized compounded Internal Rate of Return (IRR).

Mutual Funds		Mutual Funds	
Investment		Investment	
Year	Amount	Year	Amount
2007	-6,000	2007	-6,000
2008	-20,000	2008	-20,000
2009	-30,000	2009	-30,000
2010	-12,000	2010	-12,000
2011		2011	
Value as on Dec 2010	1,01,800	Value as on Dec 2010	1,01,800
IRR	=IRR(C5:C10)	IRR	18.66%

Fig 3: *Step 3 for Solution 4*

So, the annualized IRR comes out to be 18.66% which is higher than 15% from UTI mutual funds. So, it makes sense to continue to invest in Reliance mutual funds in the coming year rather than moving to UTI mutual funds.

Note that the rate of returns is annualized since each row in the above table represents an annual period which is an annual inflow or outflow.

I would like to recommend that you practice with an actual Microsoft Excel sheet if there is even an iota of doubt in your mind about the results or the way it is calculated.

I repeat, do not move ahead if you have not understood this. Go through the chapter once again if you have any doubts or log on to the website or send me an email. We will explain it to you until you are comfortable.

You have now seen some fundamental rate of return calculations and you also know which one to apply under what circumstances.

These calculations take care of the time of investment, amount of investment and the period of investment. But unfortunately, none of these calculations take into account, one of the biggest factors eating into your returns, namely "inflation". We need to know what the net rate of return is after adjusting for inflation to see and understand whether your investments are actually growing or not.

We will deal with inflation in more depth in the next few sections of the book, but at this stage it is important to understand what inflation is, how it impacts our returns and how we measure or calculate the same. The next section on Cost Inflation Index[25] (CII) essentially deals with the impact of inflation on your returns.

Technical Concepts in Financial Independence	
Evolution of Money	Cost Inflation Index
Absolute Returns	Taxes
Annualized Simple Interest Returns	Capital Gain (Loss) Tax
Compounded Annual Growth Rate (CAGR)	Dollar Cost Averaging
Internal Rate of Return (IRR)	Rule of 72
	Portfolio Asset Allocation

Cost Inflation Index

We have understood by now that the value of money decreases over a period of time due to the effect of inflation. Thus, an amount of some years back cannot be compared directly with an amount of today or with an amount in the future.

This brings me back to the point, is the rate of return that we calculated in the previous sections the actual money earned or is it just fictitious? Well the rate of return that we calculated earlier does give the actual rate of increase in "amount" of money but does not give us an actual increase in the "value" or the "purchasing power" that we have in our hands.

The reason for this is that if the running annual rate of inflation is, say, 10%, then inflation has just eaten 10% of the 18.66% annualized which we had earned through Reliance mutual funds in Solution 4. Therefore my effective increase in purchasing power is just 8.66%, meaning if I could buy 100 kg of Mangoes last year, I can afford to buy approx 109 kg this year and definitely not 119 kg.

Thus, understanding and working knowledge of how to calculate inflation across multiple years is critical.

To make any purchase price comparable to today's price, we

need to use the inflation figures from both the years and see the net difference.

Here in India, the Reserve Bank of India (RBI) has made our task easy. RBI publishes an inflation number called the Cost Inflation Index (CII) every year (starting from 1980).

The Cost inflation index by itself does not convey anything – but the increase in the number from one year to another is representative of the change in prices (and therefore, inflation) between these years.

Figure 4 provides the CII for 20 years starting from 1981. What we can see clearly, is that one had to spend ₹ 182 in 1990-91 (S.No.10) for an item which was available at ₹ 100 just 10 years prior i.e., in 1981-82 (S.No.1). The table is updated by the RBI every year based on the increase in prices of various essential commodities in that particular year.

This helps us to effectively compare returns and amounts across years after adjusting for inflation.

Cost Inflation Index

SR. NO.	FINANCIAL YEAR	COST INFLATION INDEX	SR. NO.	FINANCIAL YEAR	COST INFLATION INDEX
1.	1981-82	100	2.	1982-83	109
3.	1983-84	116	4.	1984-85	125
5.	1985-86	133	6.	1986-87	140
7.	1987-88	150	8.	1988-89	161
9.	1989-90	172	10.	1990-91	182
11.	1991-92	199	12.	1992-93	223
13.	1993-94	244	14.	1994-95	259
15.	1995-96	281	16.	1996-97	305
17.	1997-98	331	18.	1998-99	351
19.	1999-2000	389	20.	2000-01	406
21.	2001-02	426	22.	2002-03	447
23.	2003-04	463	24.	2004-05	480
25.	2005-06	497	26.	2006-07	519
27.	2007-08	551	28.	2008-09	582

Fig 4: *CII figures starting from 1980*

So, if you have got an "absolute return" of 50% on a 5 year investment from 1981 to 1986, you know that 40% of it has been eaten away by inflation and only 10% is the "actual appreciation" of your investment or your money.

Well, as long as you are able to keep your money ahead of inflation, I would say you are doing a good job, but you cannot continue to do so by keeping your money in FDs or bank savings accounts. You must make sound "investment" decisions to be able to do so.

Before we start to look at investment tools and see what options are available to us for investment and how to stay ahead of inflation, there are a few other key aspects regarding investments and returns which we must appraise ourselves with.

In the initial part of this section, we gave the definition of investment, and mentioned that it is all about keeping ahead of inflation and taxes. We have already discussed inflation and how to calculate the returns and adjust for inflation.

The other enemy of your money is the taxes[26] that you pay on your money.

In the next section we learn about the different taxes that we pay on our money and how we can reduce them.

Technical Concepts in Financial Independence	
Evolution of Money	Cost Inflation Index
Absolute Returns	**Taxes**
Annualized Simple Interest Returns	**Capital Gain (Loss) Tax**
Compounded Annual Growth Rate (CAGR)	**Dollar Cost Averaging**
Internal Rate of Return (IRR)	**Rule of 72**
	Portfolio Asset Allocation

Taxes

In layman's terms, taxes are a financial charge or other levy imposed upon a taxpayer[27] (an individual or legal entity) by a state or the functional equivalent of a state such that failure to pay is punishable by law. A tax is not a voluntary payment or donation, but an enforced contribution imposed by the government whether under the name of income, toll, tribute, duty, custom, excise, subsidy, aid, supply, or any other name. Taxes consist of direct tax or indirect tax, and may be paid in money or as its labour equivalent.

There are various categories of taxes and some of the commonly known tax categories are listed below. Taxation is a very comprehensive subject in itself and its detailed study is beyond the scope of this book. The idea of introducing this topic here is to make sure that you are familiar with the fundamental concept of taxation and its impact on your investment returns.

Tax categories

1. Taxes on income
   a. Income tax
   b. Capital gains tax
   c. Corporate tax

2. Taxes on property
   a. Property tax
   b. Transfer tax
   c. Wealth tax

3. Taxes on goods and services
   a. Sales tax

   b. Excise tax

   c. VAT

4. Other taxes
   a. License tax

   b. Toll tax

While there is a specific section towards the end of this book on income tax[28] and some smart ways to save tax on income, we will currently focus on capital gains tax which is not that common. A general understanding of the taxation structure is important to take informed decisions while making investments under various tools.

Let us start with capital gains taxes under various situations.

Technical Concepts in Financial Independence	
Evolution of Money	Cost Inflation Index
Absolute Returns	Taxes
Annualized Simple Interest Returns	**Capital Gain (Loss) Tax**
Compounded Annual Growth Rate (CAGR)	Dollar Cost Averaging
Internal Rate of Return (IRR)	Rule of 72
	Portfolio Asset Allocation

Capital Gain (Loss) Tax

A capital gain[29] is an income derived from the sale of any investment or capital asset[30]. A capital investment or a capital asset can be a home, a farm, a ranch, a family business, or a work of art, for instance.

The capital gain is the difference between the money received from selling the asset and the price paid for it.

The capital gains tax is different from almost all other forms of taxation in that it is a voluntary tax, in one way. Since the tax is paid only when an asset is sold, taxpayers can legally avoid payment by holding on to their assets — a phenomenon known as the "lock-in effect." For example, if the price of your home keeps growing, you do not have to pay a capital gains tax on the capital asset that you "still possess," but you will have to pay a capital gains tax once you sell the house, which is based on the amount you earned on this capital asset.

There is a lot of unfairness in the current tax treatment of capital gains.

Firstly, capital gains are not indexed for inflation (except for long-term capital gains tax on capital assets like a house, farm, etc). The seller pays tax not only on the real gain in purchasing power but also on the illusory gain attributable to inflation. The inflation penalty is one reason that, historically, capital gains have been taxed at lower rates than ordinary income. In fact, "most capital gains were not gains of real purchasing power at all, but simply represented the maintenance of principal in an inflationary world."

Secondly, individuals are permitted to deduct only a portion of the capital losses that they incur, whereas they must pay taxes on all of the gains. This introduces an unfriendly bias in the tax code against risk taking. When taxpayers undertake risky investments, the government taxes fully any gain that they realize if the investment has a positive return. But the government allows only partial tax deduction if the venture goes sour and results in a loss.

Thirdly, there is another large inequity of the capital gains tax.

It represents a form of double taxation on capital formation. This is how economists Victor Canto and Harvey Hirschorn explain the situation: "A government can choose to tax either the value of an asset or its yield, but it should not tax both." Capital gains are literally the appreciation in the value of an existing asset. Any appreciation reflects merely an increase in the after-tax rate of return on the asset. The taxes implicit in the asset's after-tax earnings are already fully reflected in the asset's price or change in price. Any additional tax is strictly double taxation." Take, for example, the capital gains tax paid on pharmaceutical stock. The value of the stock is based on the discounted present value of all of the future proceeds of the company. If the company is expected to earn ₹ 100,000 a year for the next 20 years, the sales price of the stock will reflect those returns. The "gain" that the seller realizes from the sale of the stock will reflect those future returns and thus the seller will pay capital gains tax on the future stream of income. But the company's future ₹ 100,000 annual returns will also be taxed when they are earned. So the ₹ 100,000 in profits is taxed twice, once when the owners sell their shares of stock and secondly when the company actually earns the income.

That is why many tax analysts argue that the most equitable rate of tax on capital gains is zero.

Long-term and short-term capital gains tax

Capital gain is classified into two types, depending on the period of holding of the capital asset.

▶ Short-Term Capital Gain (STCG)

▶ Long-Term Capital Gain (LTCG)

The taxation based on above classification also varies depending on the type of the capital asset. Let us understand this classification based on the two types of capital assets given below.

1. Shares/Stocks/MFs

2. All other capital assets

Shares/Stocks/Equities and Equity Mutual Funds (MFs)

Short-Term Capital Gain (STCG)

If shares or equity MFs are held for less than 12 months before selling, the gain arising is classified as short-term capital gain.

The only condition here is that the shares/equities should be sold on a recognized stock exchange (for example, BSE or NSE), and a Securities Transaction Tax (STT) should be paid on it. If the sale of shares is off-market (that is, if the sale is not on a stock exchange), the gain would be classified in the same way as for other capital assets.

In this case, the short-term capital gain is taxed at 15% of the gain.

Remember that a short-term capital loss arising from sale of shares can be offset against a short-term capital gain from the sale of other shares, as long as both the sales occur in the same financial year.

Long-Term Capital Gain (LTCG)

If shares or equity MFs are held for more than 12 months before selling, the gain arising is classified as Long-Term Capital Gain.

In the case of long-term capital gain arising out of the sale of shares or equity mutual funds, there is 0% income tax. The main reason for zero tax is the concept of double taxation as explained earlier.

Since the tax is zero for long-term gains, we need not worry much about the impact of inflation on the taxes.

All other capital assets

Short-Term Capital Gain (STCG)

If the capital asset is held for less than 36 months before selling, the gain arising from it is classified as short-term capital gain. This short-term capital gain is clubbed with your income for the year, and is taxed at a rate as per the applicable tax slabs/brackets. This is true even for shares or equity mutual funds sold off market. So, if you sold your house within 36 months of buying the same, all the difference between the purchase price and selling price of that house is considered as a part of your income and would be taxed as per the applicable tax slabs and rates.

At the highest tax bracket, it can be as high as 30%

Long-Term Capital Gain (LTCG)

If the capital asset is held for more than 36 months before selling, the gain arising from the sale, it is classified as long-term capital gain. In this case, 20% of the long-term capital gain has to be paid as income tax.

Since the income tax on long-term capital gains is not 0%, we need to adjust for cost inflation since the capital asset was purchased. The purchase price that needs to be used for calculating the long-term capital gains has to be matched with the equivalent price for the year in which the asset is being sold. Such an adjusted purchase price is called the Indexed Cost of Acquisition and is detailed in Formula 4.

Formula 4

Indexed Cost of Aquisition =

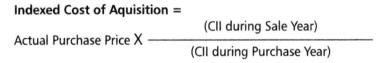

$$\text{Actual Purchase Price} \times \frac{(\text{CII during Sale Year})}{(\text{CII during Purchase Year})}$$

Here, CII represents the Cost Inflation Index[25], as studied earlier.

This formula results in inflating the purchase price and brings it at par with the current year so that the capital gain is more realistic and adjusted for inflation.

The revised formula for calculating long-term capital gains is hence derived from this updated indexed Cost of Acquisition rather than the purchase price and is as depicted in Formula 5.

Also, in case of a house, you can add the cost of any improvements (incurred during your ownership of the house) in the cost price of the house. Again, this cost can be indexed (and therefore, increased!).

Formula 5

LTCG = Sale Price – Indexed Cost of Acquisition

If your total income including the STCG or LTCG is less than the taxable threshold, you would not have to pay any STCG/LTCG tax.

If your total income excluding STCG/LTCG (A) is less than the taxable threshold, but the total income including the STCG/LTCG (B) is more than the taxable threshold, you would only have to pay STCG/LTCG tax on the excess amount (B - taxable threshold).

This gives you some idea about taxation on capital gains. Taxes on your other incomes, whether from salary or interests, are taxed as per standard taxation laws and taxable income for that year.

Since capital gains are taxed slightly differently from your other incomes, it was important to cover this topic early.

Having understood the formulae to calculate multiple types of returns and dealt with the taxes on capital gains, let us move on from these formulae to some more important technical concepts connected with investing.

It is very important to understand the investment concepts given below before getting into the details of investment tools. We will start with the concept of dollar cost averaging[31].

Technical Concepts in Financial Independence	
Evolution of Money	Cost Inflation Index
Absolute Returns	Taxes
Annualized Simple Interest Returns	Capital Gain (Loss) Tax
Compounded Annual Growth Rate (CAGR)	**Dollar Cost Averaging**
Internal Rate of Return (IRR)	Rule of 72
	Portfolio Asset Allocation

Dollar Cost Averaging

Investing in capital assets like equities/stocks is a very common investment tool and it is good to know some technical concepts for such investments. When you are ready to invest your money in equity, you will want to use a common technique called "dollar cost averaging".

With dollar cost averaging, you are investing a portion of your money at regular intervals (may be monthly) or whenever you see market dips in the equities. This averages out the price of whatever shares you are buying over time. This method of investment puts time, your money and the market on your side.

When you do this, you will be bringing down the average cost per share as you keep investing. As a rule of thumb, whenever I used to invest in equity, my thumb rule to perform dollar cost averaging has been that as and when the equity price has reduced by more than 15% of the current average cost, I would invest more to bring the average cost further down.

It is easier said than done. Below is a real life example of K S Oils (Figure 5) - one of my actual stock positions at various times along with the track of purchases I made to maximize the benefits of dollar cost averaging.

You must take a close look at the price I bought this stock for, how I kept investing as and when the stock price went down and when I felt it was drastically down, how I invested a much larger sum when the price went down further, to maximize the averaging principle.

EDIBLE OIL | INDIAN PRIVATE

K S OILS

HSL: KSOILS | BSE Code: 526209 | NSE Symbol: KSOILS | ISIN: INE727D01022

TRANSACTIONS HISTORY

Date	Buy / Sell	Exchange	Qty.	Unit Price	Trans. Amount	Type
02-06-2011	Buy	BSE	375	26.50	9,937.50	Delivery
07-08-2011	Buy	BSE	350	14.25	4,987.50	Delivery
17-08-2011	Buy	BSE	1,100	9.00	9,900.00	Delivery
17-08-2011	Buy	BSE	2,850	8.75	24,937.50	Delivery
15-09-2011	Buy	BSE	4,675	12.25	57,268.75	Delivery

Fig 5: *Dollar cost averaging for K S Oils*

1. After buying the stock (375 shares) at ₹ 26.50, I felt very confident that I had been able to purchase the stock at a very attractive price. But, as it happens many times in the stock market, you can never predict the future. The stock kept crashing because of multiple management issues in the organization.

2. Since I was continuously aware of and reading about the management issues and was fairly confident that this would not be a permanent phase in the company, I shortlisted this stock and started applying the dollar cost averaging principle here.

3. Two months after my purchase, when the stock price was almost half the price at which I purchased it, I invested

further money to bring down the average cost of purchase from ₹ 26.50 to ₹ 20.59.

4. Again, to my surprise, the stock dipped further to unimaginable values of ₹ 9 and ₹ 8.75. Some of you may get alarmed here and feel that you should be cautious of this stock and some may even start removing money from the stock at this stage fearing huge losses. This is where your knowledge of the reasons for the dip is so critical.

5. Another critical factor that had to be kept in mind was that although the stock was going down drastically, the overall market picture was also very gloomy and was also going down (though not to such a great extent).

6. Since I was confident of the long-term claw back of this stock, I took this as a welcome opportunity and invested a larger amount at this low price, thus bringing down the average cost price of the stock to a level of ₹ 10.64 (see the table on next page to understand the average costs at each step)

As expected, sooner rather than later, the management issues started to settle down, markets recovered a little bit and the stock was back to ₹ 12.25 within a month.

Now, if you compare the stock price on 15th Sep (₹ 12.25) to the original value of ₹ 26.50 (in July 2011 when I first bought the stock), I would never have been in a position to sell it off profitably at this stage. Since I exploited the concept of Dollar Cost averaging to my advantage and since I was keeping abreast of the market situation, my average purchase price for this stock was just ₹ 10.64.

Buying at an average cost of ₹ 10.64 and selling at ₹ 12.25 within 2 months, seemed lucrative enough (approx 15% returns in a period of 2 months), I decided to sell the stock at this price and pocketed a handsome annualized return of 124%.

Note that the stock was still 50% down from the original price at which I bought it but I still sold the entire amount at a handsome profit. The data in Figure 6 will help you to understand the transaction level dollar cost averaging and how it worked for this stock.

Date	Trx Type	Exchange	Quantity	Unit Price	Amount	Average Cost (Dollar Cost Averaging)
2-JUN-11	BUY	BSE	375	26.50	9,937.50	26.50
7-AUG-11	BUY	BSE	350	14.25	4,987.50	20.59
17-AUG-11	BUY	BSE	1100	9.00	9,900.00	13.60
17-AUG-11	BUY	BSE	2850	8.75	24,937.50	10.64
Total			4,675		49,762.50	

Fig 6: *Transaction level dollar cost averaging for K S Oils*

Figure 6 shows how the average cost kept coming down as I purchased more and more on stock dips, thus utilizing the concept of dollar cost averaging.

The moment I got a chance to sell at a handsome margin above the average cost price, I did so and returned with a handsome 124% CAGR (recall the CAGR and IRR formulae in the earlier sections).

Figure 7 shows the calculation of CAGR/IRR for the above stock history.

Month	Investment	Action
JUN-11	-9937	Buy
JUL-11	0	No action
AUG-11	-39825	Buy
Annual IRR	124%	Returns

Month	Investment	Action
SEP-11	57269	*Sell*
Monthly IRR	10.3%	Returns
Annual IRR	124%	Returns

Fig 7: *Returns calculation based on IRR for K S Oils*

Today, the stock is hovering around ₹ 11.05 (down more than 10% from when I sold it) and I am again looking to invest some money here.

Having said that let me also warn you that this strategy has to be carefully applied. It is easier said than done. Investing your hard earned money into a stock which is coming down and when the market mood is negative requires a very professional and long-term outlook. It is not feasible to do it with borrowed money or a faint heart.

Obviously, there are certain precautions that you must take care of. Invest only in those stocks which are going down with the market trend and not in those that fall heavily while the market is going up or is more or less flat. There may be other reasons for such stock to fall. You should also research those reasons before continuing to use this otherwise sound principle.

Remember that in any case, your long-term target when investing in equities should never be just the capital gains from the stock but a continuous positive cash flow. This will be dealt with in detail in the next sections. The aim of this section was for you to understand the concept of dollar cost averaging.

A combination of capital gains in the long run and positive cash flow during regular intervals (even during the downslide) is what has the potential to make you really rich.

Let us look at a few more technical concepts, rules and definitions in this section.

Technical Concepts in Financial Independence	
Evolution of Money	Cost Inflation Index
Absolute Returns	Taxes
Annualized Simple Interest Returns	Capital Gain (Loss) Tax
Compounded Annual Growth Rate (CAGR)	Dollar Cost Averaging
Internal Rate of Return (IRR)	**Rule of 72**
	Portfolio Asset Allocation

Rule of 72

The Rule of 72[32] gives an approximate rule to calculate how much time it takes to double your money if you know the annual rate of compounded interest.

To calculate the number of years required to double your money, divide 72 by the annual compounded rate of interest. So, if you have ₹ 10,000 in hand and want to know how soon it will double if you put it in a fixed deposit at 10% compounded rate of interest, it is as simple as 72/10 or 7.2 years.

You can apply the same rule to inflation also in order to calculate when your money's effective value would be reduced to half. The reason you can apply the same rule is that inflation is a compounded number.

As an example, if inflation is 5% an year, it will take approximately 72/5 or around 15 years for your ₹ 10,000 to be worth only ₹ 5,000.

As we have studied earlier, it is crucial to understand and study both compound interest and inflation together because your investments need to grow faster than inflation or at least be able to keep up with it.

So, what's the POINT?   Your investments need to grow faster than the Inflation

We will now learn a few concepts about a portfolio[33] and how we can allocate our investments across various asset classes[34] in the portfolio.

Technical Concepts in Financial Independence	
Evolution of Money	Cost Inflation Index
Absolute Returns	Taxes
Annualized Simple Interest Returns	Capital Gain (Loss) Tax
Compounded Annual Growth Rate (CAGR)	Dollar Cost Averaging
Internal Rate of Return (IRR)	Rule of 72
	Portfolio Asset Allocation

Portfolio Asset Allocation

Before we move to portfolio asset allocation, we must understand what an asset class is and what kind of various asset classes exist in the market today.

An asset class is defined as a group of assets or securities that exhibit similar characteristics, behave similarly in the marketplace, and are subject to the same laws and regulations.

Asset classes and asset class categories[35] are often mixed up. In other words, describing large-cap stocks or short-term bonds asset classes is incorrect. These investment vehicles are asset class categories, and are used for diversification purposes.

There is no definite way to define asset classes that is universally accepted, but most professional asset allocators agree on three major asset classes:

1. Cash deposits
2. Fixed interest
3. Equities (includes both shares and property)

Equities[36] are defined as investments that provide no security of income or capital, so the class includes both shares and property. But most advisers using asset allocation also consider property (with two distinct categorizations of residential and commercial) as a separate asset class.

For all practical purposes, we consider property (not the one you are living in but the one which you are using as an investment) as a separate asset class and therefore we have four asset classes i.e., cash deposits, fixed interest, property and shares.

Index-linked securities, commodities, gold and art are other classes or categories, and there are more obscure ones too. But for most investors, four major asset classes should be enough, because many of the other proposed separate asset classes can be considered as sub-classes or categories of these four.

Different asset classes possess different risks and yield different returns. Obviously, the greater the risk[37] you are ready to take, the greater your chances of handsome returns. Figure 8 gives a summary of the risk rewards for various asset classes.

Asset class	Volatility	Returns
Cash deposits		●
Fixed Interest	●	● ●
Property	● ● ●	● ● ●
Shares	● ● ● ● ●	● ● ● ●

Fig 8: *Risk reward for various asset classes*

Once you know the asset classes, the question arises as to how much money to invest in which investment vehicle or asset class. This completely depends on your risk appetite[38] and the time period in which you are looking at the return on your investment.

How you divide your investments between stocks (shares) and bonds, equity and debt, and low rate of return vs high rate of return – is the single most important concept for building a secure retirement plan. Over the years, you need different types of investment vehicles to reach your goals, and you need them in different proportions.

Portfolio asset allocation[39] (also called asset allocation) is an investment planning technique that allows you to get the right balance between risk and return by investing in a variety of assets. Remember, that there is no specific rule of thumb on portfolio asset allocation, though there are many theories on how to allocate your money to different asset classes. This process of allocating your assets in different proportions to make your custom portfolio is your personal choice.

Asset allocation is a method of investment planning that aims to maximize the returns for any given level of risk, or reduce the risk for any given level of return, by allocating capital to different types of assets in suitable proportions. It is based on observations showing that different asset classes have very typical patterns of returns and price variations over long periods of time.

This methodology is a somewhat sophisticated extension of the old adage, 'don't put all your eggs in one basket', which inevitably prompts the question, 'which baskets should I put them in, and how many in each?'

To make asset allocation work for you, all you really need is a little common sense, not high level mathematics.

Warren Buffett, the world's richest investor and second richest man, has many times said that he thinks 'high school math' is the most any investor needs, and that the more complicated the math, the less useful for the investor.

The right way to use asset allocation is to keep it simple. Common sense is right — picking great investments is what will make you rich. What asset allocation will do is prevent you losing a lot of money through over-optimism or carelessness. It is a reality check, a risk control device designed to help you grow rich slowly but steadily.

There are many techniques and rules of thumb in the market. We are not going into detail about any of these techniques in this book, as this is a separate subject in itself.

A general rule of thumb for equities is that the content of equities in your portfolio should be 100 minus your age. The rest of the investments can go into fixed income debt based investments. Remember that equities include both shares and your property investments, and property investment does not include the house where you are currently living.

This "100 minus" rule sounded ridiculous to me, and much too high, when I started investing in equities.

Why invest in equities at all? Simply because they have proven time and again (and definitely in the last 30-40 years) that they yield the maximum returns on your invested money as long as you have a long-term outlook.

This 100 minus rule essentially means that you should invest more in equities when you are young and keep reducing the same as you go along. Why so? Well, it is actually very logical, as equities are volatile. They go up and down faster than fixed interest investments. Thus, a stock market crash can temporarily wipe out your savings. While you are young, this may not be a big concern as you have time on your hands. On the other hand, this may not be a particularly good situation to be in, when you are nearing your retirement.

Figure 9 gives you a typical break up of asset allocation. The asset allocation in Figure 9 looks like a very conservative portfolio asset allocation since only 30% + 10% = 40% is allocated to equities (shares + real estate). Again, the asset class break up is a very personal choice and you may or may not follow any rules.

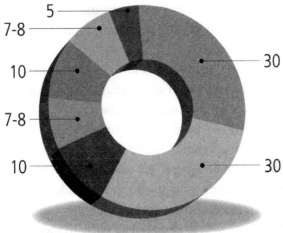

EQUITY
Return expectations for 2011 subdued due to high current valuations, inflation outlook and the possibility of higher interest rates. Year for stock selection.

FIXED INCOME
With interest rates headed up, fixed deposits and debt funds can give returns rivalling stocks. Wait for government borrowing data and RBI rate moves.

REAL ESTATE
Property prices are back to pre-crash levels. Overall markets will remain sluggish. Specific opportunities in redevelopment and premium properties will open up.

GOLD & SILVER
Abundant cash in the global markets and the prospect of geopolitical tensions to keep precious metals in demand. Silver may outperform gold.

COMMODITIES
Prices to rise. Food demand in India and China fuelling the rise. Demand-supply situation tightening. Chinese slowdown could lead to a correction.

ART
There is steam left in the recovery in art prices. The effect of economic slowdown and a sluggish equity market could soften prices.

PRIVATE EQUITY
Opportunities in segments not available through public markets. Financial inclusion businesses are hot favourites. Highly illiquid investment.

Fig 9: *A typical conservative portfolio asset allocation*

In most cases, you should stick to these fundamental rules so that you need not worry about which direction the stock market is going on a day to day basis.

This brings us to the end of this section. Spend enough time; go through the concepts and definitions again till you are absolutely clear about them.

I had a hard time understanding all these concepts and had to break my head over various magazines, journals, websites and newspapers to arrive at these definitions and conclusions. I want you to take full benefit of my learning and understand these concepts and definitions. As you move on through your journey, these concepts will be extremely useful. I have tried to keep these as simple as I can. If you still have any questions, you can log on to our website at http://www.ratrace2freedom.com

Since you now have a basic understanding of the technical concepts, you are now ready to look at the spectrum of investment tools that are available and which you can utilize for your investments.

3

Financial Investment Tools

Academic qualifications are important and so is financial education. They're both important and schools are forgetting one of them.

— Robert Kiyosaki

Having learnt some of the most fundamental concepts about money, calculation of returns and allocation of assets, it is time to start looking at some of the tools available in the market that you can utilize to actually start investing your money and start the learning process on your journey to financial freedom.

As you go through these tools, do not forget the end objective, which is to have enough in your nest egg[40], so that the money can take care of itself. Once the nest egg becomes large and strong enough, you can term yourself truly "free" for that is when you can fulfil your bigger dreams of life. Always remember that building this nest egg should be a means to achieve bigger goals and dreams in life, and not an end itself, if you want to achieve true happiness.

There are so many investment options available today across all the asset classes that it can become confusing, at times, to decide where to invest, how much to invest and when to invest.

This section will give you an overview of the many financial investment tools that I have personally invested in. However, the list is by no means exhaustive or complete. There are certain financial investment tools like art, coin and stamp collections, in which I have very limited exposure, but they seem to have a good future potential. Such tools are not covered in this book for the simple reason that I lack personal experience in investing in them and it would not be fair to recommend anything that I have not experienced myself.

Also, considering the fact that this book is aimed at motivating people about the importance of financial freedom and getting them started on this extremely critical journey of their lives, it is assumed that these relatively "rarer" financial investment tools like art, etc., will come as a regular learning experience for budding financially free professionals.

This book just "keeps things simple" and "gets you started". After that, it is all in your hands.

Some of the investment tools that we will be discussing in this section are given below.

Financial Investment Tools	
Bank Fixed Deposits (FDs)	Stocks
Bank Recurring Deposits (RDs)	Bonds
PPF (Public Provident Fund)	Mutual Funds
EPF (Employee Provident Fund)	FMPs (Fixed Maturity Plans) of MFs
VPF (Voluntary Provident Fund)	Commodities
Gratuity	Life Insurance
Superannuation	Real Estate
Gold	

We will start with the first and the most widely known investment tool i.e., bank fixed deposits.

Financial Investment Tools	
Bank Fixed Deposits (FDs)	Stocks
Bank Recurring Deposits (RDs)	Bonds
PPF (Public Provident Fund)	Mutual Funds
EPF (Employee Provident Fund)	FMPs (Fixed Maturity Plans) of MFs
VPF (Voluntary Provident Fund)	Commodities
Gratuity	Life Insurance
Superannuation	Real Estate
Gold	

Bank Fixed Deposits (FDs)

This is one of the most easiest short-term investment strategies and planning tools available in your portfolio. Not only are your investments relatively safe with fixed deposits, but you will also have the liquidity to encash them at your will.

The term fixed deposit[41] refers to an investment method where you can deposit money in a financial institution to earn interest for the life of investment period. It is called a fixed deposit because the investment period is fixed at the start of the investment. Fixed deposits are also called term deposits[41] or time deposits[41] in the US and bonds in the UK.

A fixed deposit is considered to be the lazy man's investment method because the risk involved is almost zero. It is also the safest and most secure form of investment. Your money is deposited in the safest place, i.e., the banks[42].

When you invest your money in a fixed deposit, your money is working for you even while you sleep. Your money is like an employee (or a slave) whom you do not have to pay a monthly salary to. It will work to make more money until the fixed deposit tenure is over.

The important characteristics of a fixed deposit are the rate of return (interest rate) and the investment time period. A certificate of deposit is a legally binding agreement between you and the financial institution about these characteristics.

Advantages of a fixed deposit

Fixed deposits have several benefits over other investment methods.

Some of these are:

1. **Your money is safe**

   Your deposits are safe in banks. These deposits are insured under the Deposit Insurance and Credit Guarantee

Scheme of India. This means that in a catastrophe, you will get your money back from the government.

2. No risk is involved

Fixed deposits are more suitable for small investors and even for beginners, because risk is not a factor. As the market fluctuations never affect fixed deposit, you can earn a steady income from this type of investment.

3. Depositing and withdrawal procedure is simple

You can start a fixed deposit with a small amount, may be as small as 500 rupees. You just have to fill out the required forms and hand over the money to get the certificate of deposit in a matter of minutes. Internet banking even allows you to do the same much faster from the comfort of your home. The withdrawal procedure is also simple. You just have to hand over the signed Certificate of Deposit (CD) to the banker and your money will be deposited to your savings bank account.

I personally use the online method of creating new fixed deposits with an option to auto refund to my savings account as soon as the fixed deposit matures. It is a real time/instant method of FD creation where you chose the time period, (and hence interest rates), amount, bank, branch etc., and then you get an FD advice in your email with a click of a button. I use this feature regularly for most known banks where I have accounts like HDFC Bank, ICICI Bank, State Bank of India.

4. Guaranteed returns

When you open a fixed deposit account, you are signing up for a fixed return scheme. This means, your financial institution has to provide your fixed returns under any economic conditions during the tenure period. In addition to this, the financial institution is obliged to return your money on the maturity date including any interest as agreed up on.

5. **Higher interest than a savings account**

If your savings account has extra money, it is wise to invest in fixed deposits, as the rate of return is higher. Some banks even offer a zero balance on your savings account when you start a fixed deposit with them.

You should also check whether your bank has a facility to automatically convert your savings deposits, beyond a threshold value, into fixed deposits and breaking your fixed deposits automatically if there is a need of funds in the savings account. Such flexible accounts are common and easily available on request.

6. **Loan availability**

You can avail of loans against a fixed deposit in case of financial difficulties. According to RBI regulations, the banks can allow up to 75 to 90% of the fixed deposit as a loan amount. The interest rate you have to pay for taking such loans will be just 2% higher than what you get from the investment.

7. **Premature withdrawal**

Unlike mutual funds and other fixed investment schemes, financial institutions allow you to withdraw funds from a fixed deposit before reaching the maturity period. Some banks may charge you a minimum penalty if you withdraw money before the minimum investment period is completed.

8. **Varied deposit options**

   In addition to banks and other banking financial institutions, fixed deposit accounts can be opened with housing loan financial institutions and corporations. It should be noted that the terms might be different with corporations. So it is important to read their terms before opting for corporate fixed deposits.

9. **Nominations facilities available**

   Since the fixed deposit is an investment scheme, nomination facilities are available to make sure your money will reach your loved ones even if something happens to you.

10. **Look for special interest rates**

    Most banks offer special interest rates on fixed deposits for special "odd" periods of deposits for multiple reasons. As an example, it is common to see an 8% interest on a 1 year or a 2 year deposit scheme but the bank may also give you a 9% rate on a 375 or a 380 day deposit. You should cash in on such opportunities. In fact most of my money locked in FDs is under such special schemes, which are easily available on line.

    The reason for such special rates is not difficult to understand. We all know that the bank loans our money out at a higher rate of interest than they give us. If a bank wants to loan our money to its own customers for a one year period and is short of funds, it would encourage you to lock the money in bank FDs by providing you a higher interest rate and would take an additional 15-20 days for its loan reimbursement and collection procedures. This is a golden opportunity for someone who is trying to build wealth as none of us would mind keeping the money in the bank for additional 15 to 20 days if it provides us a 1% higher rate of interest on the entire tenure of investment.

Most financial analysts term fixed deposits as an "inefficient" way to invest your money, and I agree that there are inherent disadvantages in putting all your money in a fixed deposit scheme.

Disadvantages of fixed deposits

1. Better forms of investments are available

Stocks, bonds, mutual funds and commodities are riskier investment options, but they also provide better returns on investment. So if you are ready to take some risk, investing in these products is more sensible than investing in fixed deposits. Moreover, the risk in these options reduces as you learn more and plan better for your financial freedom.

Practically, it makes sense to invest a good part of your money in securities, other than fixed deposits and savings deposits, because of inflation. If you have to beat inflation, you need to be efficient about allocating your investments in the right investment tools and spreading them across to even out the risks. If you do not do that, your standard of living will keep going down, although your money in "absolute" terms is going up.

One of the biggest ironies in life is that most of us are extremely good in whatever planning we do at our jobs and businesses. On the other hand, we do not even know what annualized returns we are getting from all the investments that we make. We have no clue whether our investments will be able to beat inflation year on year or not. If we do not even know that, how can we take an informed decision?

It all comes down to the risk reward ratio. The back bone of any investment strategy is to at least beat the running inflation (after taxes) and then maximize returns on the invested amount. If a fixed deposit cannot help you beat inflation, you must seriously consider other options.

2. **Returns are taxable**

The interest you earn from fixed deposits is fully taxable. Thus, you have to show these returns as your income when you file your income tax returns. Some banks deduct TDS from these returns if you fail to add your PAN card details.

Comparing it with a safer long-term investment option like PPF, this is a very big disadvantage of fixed deposits. If you are in the higher income bracket, and you get 30% of your FD returns wiped out in taxes, it no longer leaves FD as a very good investment option. Assuming you earn even a 9% return on a 1 year fixed deposit with the current inflation being 7%, then after tax deduction, the returns are likely to be less than 6%, (which is less than the inflation recovery). This essentially means you are losing money if it continues to be kept in a fixed deposit.

3. **Corporate fixed deposits are not always safe**

Some companies other than banking institutions also offer fixed deposits, but they may not be entirely safe. They do offer higher rates of interest as compared to banking institutions. This is because they are likely to invest your money in the projects that they have planned and get enough Return On Investment (ROI) from their projects to pay you the interest as well as earn profits.

There is a chance of bankruptcy, which may result in

loss of your money. So you should be careful, when you invest in corporate fixed deposits.

4. Governed by the Reserve/Federal bank guidelines

The Reserve Bank of India is responsible for all monitory policies including the base lending rate[43]. The base lending rate is the rate at which banks borrow money from the Reserve Bank of India[44] or other similar central banks in their respective countries. During a strong economic period, the RBI increases the base lending rate to bring down the economy. A higher base lending rate would mean that the banks cannot loan out money at lower rates and that lowers the economy further (as there are less borrowers of money from the bank at higher rates). This controls inflation as well and is often used to bring down spiralling inflation rates.

A higher base lending rate also means that the bank can pass on the benefits to you as a retail investor as well. Therefore, this base lending rate is directly proportional to the interest rate you will get from a fixed deposit.

By the same analogy, in a weak economic situation, the reverse is true, which essentially means that the base lending rate or the interest rate may come down to encourage big clients to borrow more money for their businesses at a lesser lending rate. This, essentially, again directly impacts the interest rate that the bank can give you on your fixed deposits.

This change of base lending rates (which is essentially counted in basis points e.g., a 3% base lending rate by the RBI would mean 300 basis points) and indicates the base lending rate that banks must use to loan money to large businesses for investments. In turn, they may decide their FD rates for retail customers.

Though this base lending rate change may hardly impact the existing fixed deposits, it will definitely impact future fixed deposits, and becomes an important factor when deciding on FDs as a long-term option.

In nutshell, if you feel that the economy is doing very well and the reserve or federal bank is increasing the base lending rate consistently, you may want to invest in a longer term fixed deposit (may be 3 to 5 years) so that you can secure a fixed high rate of return on your fixed deposit.

Does it make sense to break an old FD and invest in a new one?

Breaking an FD means premature withdrawal of your money locked into an FD – you break an FD when you take out the money before the term of the FD is over.

If the interest rates on the fixed deposits increase very rapidly, do you think it is wise to break an existing fixed deposit with a lower rate of return and invest the money in a new fixed deposit with a higher rate of return? For example, a one year bank fixed deposit that was fetching 7-7.50% 6 months back now fetches 8.50-9%. So what should you do as a retail investor?

Although it may seem that it is wise to go ahead and break an FD and reinvest the money in a new FD with a higher rate of return, you should take into account the following penalties that the banking institution may levy on you for "breaking an FD," and then arrive at a decision:

5. **Reduced interest rate**

   The first penalty is in the form of a reduced interest rate on the existing FD. When you break an FD, banks do not give the rate of interest at which you invested in the FD

– you get the rate existing at the time of starting a fixed deposit and applicable for the duration for which you actually kept the money with the bank.

This may sound rather confusing, so let us understand it better through an example.

Suppose you kept an FD for 4 years, with an interest rate of 8%. Now, you want to break it after 2 years. In this case, what interest rate would you get? You would get the rate applicable to a 2 year FD prevailing at the time when you had invested in the FD, and not the interest rate of 8% which was applicable to a 4 year FD.

So, if the rate for 2 years was 7.25% when you had invested in your 4 year FD, you would only get an interest of 7.25% per year for the 2 years you have kept the money with the bank – and not 8% per annum.

6. **Penalty in the rate of interest**

But it doesn't stop at that – most banks also charge a penalty in interest rate, which is 0.5% to 1% (there may be exceptions, which need to be discussed with the bank on a case to case basis). When you break an FD, banks normally give you an interest rate that is lower by 0.5%-1% than the interest rate applicable to an FD of the duration for which you have kept the money with the bank.

Let us continue our previous example to understand this better.

If the rate for a 2 year FD was 7.25% when you invested in your 4 year FD, and if the penalty is 1%, you would actually get an interest of 6.25% per year for the 2 years you have kept the money with the bank (and not 7.25% or 8%).

Considering the above penalties and reduced interest rates, it may be wise to calculate on a case to case basis to decide whether it is worth "breaking an FD" and investing in a new fixed deposit or waiting for your FD to mature.

In general, the following thumb rules may help you to take a decision:

a. Breaking the FD and reinvesting the sum in a higher-interest earning FD is positive only when the original FD is relatively newer – in this case, the penalty is not very high. If the original FD is old or nearing maturity, it is best to continue with it and reinvest the money only when it matures.

b. If the difference in the rate of interest between the two fixed deposits is very high i.e., the new fixed deposit is offering you almost double the existing rate of the old fixed deposit, you should do the exact calculation for your case.

In general, it is rarely worth the effort of "breaking an FD" and going in for a new one just for the sake of a higher rate of interest.

Financial Investment Tools	
Bank Fixed Deposits (FDs)	Stocks
Bank Recurring Deposits (RDs)	Bonds
PPF (Public Provident Fund)	Mutual Funds
EPF (Employee Provident Fund)	FMPs (Fixed Maturity Plans) of MFs
VPF (Voluntary Provident Fund)	Commodities
Gratuity	Life Insurance
Superannuation	Real Estate
Gold	

Bank Recurring Deposits (RDs)

Though fixed deposits are the most popular cash based investment tools, there is an alternative version of fixed deposits called recurring deposits[45]. Under a Recurring Deposit account (RD account), a specific amount is invested in a bank on a monthly basis for a fixed rate of return. The deposit has a fixed tenure, at the end of which the principal sum as well as the interest earned during that period is returned to the investor.

A recurring deposit account makes it compulsory to save at high rates of interest applicable to term deposits along with liquidity to access those savings any time.

Since a recurring deposit offers a fixed rate of return, it does not provide protection against inflation. But this kind of account is good for those who are not in the habit of regular savings and are just beginning on their journey to financial freedom.

There is great flexibility in the period of deposit with maturity ranging from 6 months to 120 months. The minimum monthly deposit varies from bank to bank. In most of the public sector banks, one can start a recurring deposit account with a monthly instalment as small as ₹ 100/-. There is no upper limit on investing. At the time of writing this book, the rate of interest for RDs varied between 7 and 11 percent depending on the maturity period. Loan/Overdraft facilities are also available against recurring bank deposits.

The deposit for RD account is paid in monthly instalments and each subsequent monthly instalment has to be made before the end of the calendar month and is equal to the first deposit. In case of default in payment, a penalty is levied for delayed deposit at the rate of ₹ 1.50/- for every ₹ 100/- per month, for deposits up to 5 years and ₹ 2/- per ₹ 100/- in case of longer maturities. These numbers may vary for different banks.

In the case of a recurring deposit being closed before completing the original term of the deposit, interest will be paid at the rate applicable on the date of deposit, for the period for which the deposit has remained with the bank. Premature withdrawal is also permissible but penalty is levied. Tax Deduction at Source[46] (TDS) is not applicable on recurring deposits.

Financial Investment Tools	
Bank Fixed Deposits (FDs)	Stocks
Bank Recurring Deposits (RDs)	Bonds
PPF (Public Provident Fund)	Mutual Funds
EPF (Employee Provident Fund)	FMPs (Fixed Maturity Plans) of MFs
VPF (Voluntary Provident Fund)	Commodities
Gratuity	Life Insurance
Superannuation	Real Estate
Gold	

PPF (Public Provident Fund)

A Public Provident Fund[47] (PPF) is one of the simplest long-term investment strategies and planning tool available in your portfolio. Not only are your investments safe in a PPF but they also earn a high interest rate.

An extremely important fact is that the interest earned through PPF savings is not taxable. All these factors coupled together make it the safest and the most viable savings option to start investing in. I believe that the PPF was started by the Government of India in lieu of the social security system that exists in the United States and other developed countries. (I doubt if a government can ever provide social security to a billion plus people in India.)

When I started working with Larsen and Toubro Limited, I was posted in Baroda (Gujarat) in 1995. I was fortunate enough to have been guided by my supervisor and my boss at a very young age (23 years) to open a PPF account and start making small but regular and disciplined investments into it. Although I never understood the importance of such investments at that stage of my life, I still went ahead and followed my boss's advice and opened a PPF account.

I started investing ₹ 2000 per month (on the day I got my salary, which was approximately ₹ 10000 at that stage, in the year 1996). I continued investing consistently for a few years till the so called challenging situations in my life made me stop for the next 10 years. I kept withdrawing from my PPF account in between to meet my family's needs, till I was finally enlightened, around the year 2007, on the importance of financial independence and how we can all achieve it.

That small step has shaped my financial independence goals of today.

How to open a PPF account

A PPF account can be opened at the local post office – either at the head post office in your district or selected grade sub post offices. It can also be opened at your nearest select nationalized banks like the State Bank of India. However, you can have only one PPF account in your name.

Limitations of a PPF account

A PPF account has some restrictions as compared to a normal savings account:

▶ At any stage, if it is found that you have more than one

PPF account, then the account opened at a later date would be closed and only the principal amount (not the interest) would be refunded to you.

▶ You cannot have a joint PPF account, it can only be opened in your name.

▶ Non Resident Indians (NRIs) earning an income in India can also open a PPF account. Contributions, however, have to be made from a Non Resident Ordinary (NRO) account.

▶ There is a minimum lock-in period[48] of 5 years and none of the invested money can be withdrawn prior to that. Even after the 5th year, a maximum of 50% of the amount invested in Year 1 can be withdrawn. You cannot make more than one withdrawal in a financial year. This does impose constraints on your liquidity if you are a mature investor but in the initial stages of your journey, I feel this is a very critical process because you are getting into the habit of letting your money grow and multiply in a compounding manner.

▶ You must invest a minimum of ₹ 500 in each financial year in a PPF account. In case you miss out on one financial year, you are penalized for the same.

▶ The maximum investment that can be done in a PPF account in one financial year is ₹ 1, 00,000/-. My suggestion to my readers would be to reach this annual investment limit as soon as possible in the year since a PPF is one of the safest investment options. It also has extremely good returns, which are completely tax free.

Looking at the distinct advantages of a PPF account, especially for beginners, the above limitations seem to be trivial. In fact, limitations like a lock in period serve as a blessing in disguise to promote what I call the "super power of compounded money."

Benefits of investing in a PPF

▸ The money invested is perfectly safe.

▸ The investment earns a considerable interest (as compared to FDs and regular savings account). The interest rates may vary from year to year but generally are between 8 to 10%.

▸ All investments made in a PPF qualify for tax rebate under Section 80C of the IT Act.

▸ PPF investments are Exempt Exempt Exempt (EEE) – the money you invest, the interest earned, and the final withdrawable amount are all tax exempt. This actually leads to an effective interest rate which is much higher than 8 to 10% as compared to FDs and other bank deposits where everything is taxable.

To conclude, a PPF is one of the safest investments and one of the best investment vehicles for any beginners on their journey to financial freedom. It gets you into the habit of saving and yields handsome, tax free, compounded returns. They score over fixed deposits or recurring deposits in terms of returns. You just have to take the effort to open an account and start depositing money.

People were often too lazy to go to a bank and deposit money physically as nationalized banks (especially for PPF accounts) did not have on line transaction facilities. However, now it is possible to successfully deposit money in a PPF account using online banking. So it is not difficult to invest the full quota of ₹ 1,00,000 per annum in a PPF account from the comfort of your home.

Financial Investment Tools	
Bank Fixed Deposits (FDs)	Stocks
Bank Recurring Deposits (RDs)	Bonds
PPF (Public Provident Fund)	Mutual Funds
EPF (Employee Provident Fund)	FMPs (Fixed Maturity Plans) of MFs
VPF (Voluntary Provident Fund)	Commodities
Gratuity	Life Insurance
Superannuation	Real Estate
Gold	

EPF (Employee Provident Fund)

I am sure you feel disgruntled when you look at your salary slip and find that sundry deductions have pared it down. But believe me, you should actually feel happy about one of these deductions - the monthly contribution to the Employees' Provident Fund[49] (EPF), commonly called the Provident Fund[49] (PF).

If you are salaried, there is no way you would not have heard of the Provident Fund (PF). In fact, there is no way that you would not have invested in it, because it is a compulsory investment for all salaried people (PF is compulsory if you work for a company having 20 or more employees). PF is a long-term investment, even longer term than PPF. It is one of the lowest risk investment avenues, as it is backed by the government, so is as safe as PPF.

The 12% of your basic salary that flows into the EPF every month alone has the potential to make you a millionaire when you retire.

This may sound unbelievable, as the investment seems too small and the interest rate offered does not seem too high. But do not forget that a matching contribution comes from your employer every month. In fact, this happens to be the most ignored and yet the most powerful fact in company PF investments. Do not underestimate the power of compounding and what it can do to your retirement savings in the long-term. The 8.5% to 9.5% interest earned on the EPF can help a person with a basic salary of Rs 25,000 a month accumulate a gargantuan ₹ 1.65 crores in 35 years.

In fact, the EPF can single-handedly account for the debt portion of your financial portfolio. You need not invest in tax inefficient fixed deposits or worry about which debt fund to invest in. All you need to ensure is that you do not ever withdraw from your EPF account till you hang up your boots. If at any stage you find that your debt portion is lagging, you can add more through a voluntary increase in your contribution (covered in the section on VPF later).

However, few people are able to reach even the ₹ 1 crore milestone in their careers. EPF rules allow encashment of the accumulated corpus when a person leaves a job and it is not uncommon for people to withdraw their PF at that stage. I have done it myself as I moved jobs. I have taken this withdrawal as bonus money for my hard work in the job and I thought I could now make full use of the money without realizing the fact that I had just taken it out from one of the safest and best rewarding investment tools. I never realized the harm that I was doing to myself with this withdrawal. I was not financially knowledgeable at that stage and I never had the good fortune of reading books on financial freedom.

This is despite the fact that the government discourages you from withdrawing the money. The withdrawals from the EPF within five years of joining are taxable. The tax will be minimal if the person is jobless and has no significant income from other sources but you will not completely escape the tax net. When you withdraw your PPF, you forego the power of compounding.

Instead of withdrawing money from the EPF on switching jobs, one should transfer the balance to the new account with the new employer. This does not happen automatically. You need to fill a 'Form 13' and deposit it with the EPF Office[50] (EPFO). Financial advisers recommend that you put this down among the list of priorities at your new workplace. You should take up the matter with the new organization as soon as you join. Many good organizations set this up for you as a part of the on boarding process that they follow. I did this myself when I moved from TCS to IBM in 2006 and I was offered Form 13 as a part of the on boarding pack of forms. That made my job a little easier, but I still needed to fill up the form and send it to the correct destination i.e., the EPFO office. With passage of time you might get busy. Also, if your previous organization has lost the records because of too long a period, you could face a hard time looking for your PF details.

This is one of the least thought about investment tools for people in regular jobs. Since the amount gets deducted every month, the amount of money and the cumulative interest that you accumulate can be substantial in this section of your portfolio.

According to the EPF scheme, both the employee and the employer contribute at 12% of the employee's wages, DA and retaining allowance to the fund, every month. This fund gets added to the employee's EPF account and the whole amount is given to him, when he or she requires it, e.g., retirement, medical expenditures, housing costs, family obligations, education of children, paying insurance premiums, etc.

The rate of interest that you earn on your PF investment is fixed by the Central Government every year in March/April. The rate of interest changes every year, but it is usually higher than the prevailing market rates.

The employee ends up paying to his EPF every month while the interest rate on his investment is calculated in the month of

March/April every year. The applied interest rate is fixed by the ruling government of India in consultation with a central board of trustees and other concerned members. The EPF amount increases every year with the interest sum and deposited amount.

Checking the status of an EPF

The concerned department sends a statement of the EPF account to the contributing employees. The statement contains all the necessary information such as the opening balance, amount contributed in the current financial year, total interest amount earned in the current year, withdrawn amount from the fund (if applicable) etc.

Figure 10 shows what a typical EPF statement looks like:

Account Number		Name		The Employee's Provident Fund Scheme, 1952 Rate of Interest : 8.5%					
xxxxxx		xxxxxx		For the Year :					
Opening Balance Rs.		Interest Rs.		Contribution During the Year		Refund of withdrawal	Withdrawals during the year	Closing Balance Rs.	
Employee's	Employer's	Employee's	Employer's	Employee's	Employer's			Employee's	Employer's
xx	xx	xx	xx	xx	xx	xx	xx	xx	xx
						For REGIONAL PROVIDENT FUND COMMISSIONER, BANGALORE			

Fig 10: *EPF statement*

Withdrawing EPF funds

An EPF fund has been designed to help employees with some financial benefits upon his or her retirement. A contributing employee can withdraw the deposited amount completely, once he/she retires from service at the age of 55 years.

However, there are a few other options and ways that the employee can withdraw EPF funds even before retirement. One can withdraw any amount of up to 90% of the accrued amount if he or she is more than 54 years old.

On the other hand, one member is entitled to withdraw the full amount if:

1. He or she leaves India and settles abroad.

2. He/She retires from the job before reaching the 55 year age limit.

3. The person retires because of mental infirmity or in case of individual or mass retrenchment.

Key features of an EPF account

▶ An EPF is a long-term investment. It is one of the lowest risk investment avenues, as it is backed by the government.

▶ There is an equal contribution made by the employer matching the employee's contribution (up to a limit of 12%).

▶ The amount you have invested, the amount that your company has invested on your behalf and the interest earned on these amounts is absolutely tax-free if you have worked for a minimum of 5 years. If you have not worked for at least five years, but the PF has been transferred to the new employer, then too it is not taxed if the total tenure across the companies is at least 5 years.

▶ The amount you invest is eligible for deduction under the amount limit of Section 80C.

▶ Employees can take a loan against the amount accumulated in the fund. However availing of loans depends on permissible rules and circumstances and they can access money for reasons such as housing, marriage, children's education etc.

Financial Investment Tools

Bank Fixed Deposits (FDs)	Stocks
Bank Recurring Deposits (RDs)	Bonds
PPF (Public Provident Fund)	Mutual Funds
EPF (Employee Provident Fund)	FMPs (Fixed Maturity Plans) of MFs
VPF (Voluntary Provident Fund)	Commodities
Gratuity	Life Insurance
Superannuation	Real Estate
Gold	

VPF (Voluntary Provident Fund)

We have just seen that a provident fund is a mandatory arrangement by which you contribute 12% of your basic salary and the employer contributes an equal amount. On this total amount, you get a secure annual return of 8 to 10%.

However, it is possible to invest more than the mandatory 12% into your PF account and get great returns on it. Not many persons have heard about this, if you haven't, then welcome to the relatively unknown world of Voluntary Provident Fund[51] (VPF).

VPF is a safe option wherein you can contribute an amount over and above the EPF ceiling of 12% that has been mandated by the government. This additional amount enjoys all the benefits of a PF except that the employer is not liable to contribute any extra amount apart from the mandated 12%.

An added advantage is that the interest rate is equal to the interest rate of a PF and the withdrawal is tax free. The money invested in a VPF is also subject to tax relief under Section 80C[52], as in the case of 12% EPF money. The interest rate that you receive for the VPF amount is the same as what you get from the government for the EPF amount (normally 8%). The withdrawal on retirement is also tax-free.

The maximum contribution you can make towards EPF + VPF together is 100% of your basic salary and Dearness Allowance (DA).

If you would like to invest in such a scheme, you need to instruct the payroll department of your organization to deduct a pre-decided rate over the mandatory 12%, every month. This will go into your VPF. It is left to you as the employee to decide whether you would want to go in for a VPF and how much over 12% (which can be up to 100% of your basic salary and DA), you want to invest. But your organization will contribute an amount matching only the 12%.

Apart from the higher interest rates, VPF can give you a tax benefit under section 80C of the Income Tax Act. Your investments in VPF will be considered equivalent to your investment in any other investment instruments under Section 80C.

However, the downside is that while you get good risk-free returns, you should be prepared to have your money locked in, till the time of your retirement. This can be a disadvantage for a mature investor, but a blessing for someone who is just starting to learn to invest.

In case you make a premature withdrawal from your PF account, (which holds both your EPF and VPF contributions) you will have to pay taxes on this withdrawal amount.

Even then, it is still better than bank fixed deposits, where the interest paid is fully taxable.

Why is it so unheard of?

You may question the fact that when everything about a VPF seems so positive, why is so little heard of it? The reason is that although VPF sounds very promising theoretically, PF managers of companies claim that there are roadblocks in terms of infrastructural constraints.

If the organization has an arrangement with the government to manage a PF, the difficulty is lack of computerization and a problem with maintaining records. Many PF accounts are managed by EPFO, but if your PF is managed through a company trust, it may not sound like a very attractive idea for your company trust to pay about 9% to 9.5% on your VPF, more so, if you do not have an upper ceiling to it, i.e. you can invest up to 100% of your basic salary and DA and retaining allowance, if any.

Therefore, most organizations underplay the idea of VPF. Companies usually do not encourage their employees because it would mean a higher interest cost for the trust.

Benefits of VPF

▶ Employees can take a loan against the amount accumulated in the PF (VPF+EPF) fund. However availing of loans depends on permissible rules and circumstances. They can access money for reasons such as housing, marriage, children's education etc.

▶ VPF can give you a tax benefit under section 80C of the Income Tax Act.

▶ During withdrawal, both the principal and the interest are tax free.

Limitations of VPF

▶ If the employer contributes in excess of 12% towards your provident fund (which the employer rarely does), then the employee will have to pay tax on that amount.

▶ You should be prepared to have your money locked in, till the time of your retirement, or emergency needs as described earlier.

Financial Investment Tools	
Bank Fixed Deposits (FDs)	Stocks
Bank Recurring Deposits (RDs)	Bonds
PPF (Public Provident Fund)	Mutual Funds
EPF (Employee Provident Fund)	FMPs (Fixed Maturity Plans) of MFs
VPF (Voluntary Provident Fund)	Commodities
Gratuity	Life Insurance
Superannuation	Real Estate
Gold	

Gratuity

Are you rueing your decision not to change jobs, while your peers moved more than two or three times to jobs with higher salaries? However, patience can be very rewarding in financial terms. If you have completed at least five years of service, you are eligible for a lump-sum payment in the form of gratuity[53] when you finally bid farewell to a company. Your former colleagues, who changed every two or three years for lucrative new offers, will not be eligible for the same benefit.

Gratuity is one of the oldest employee-retention tools used by HR managers. It used to be one of the three major retirement benefits along with the Employees' Provident Fund and pension. The objective was to make it lucrative for an employee to stay in the company in the long-term and reap benefits. But unlike the retention bonuses that companies now offer to select employees, gratuity used to be for all employees in a company.

However, gratuity has lost favour over the years because job-hopping has become the norm. The average employee now changes jobs every 2-4 years. I myself changed 6 jobs in 15 years, before I settled down for more than 5 years in my last job with IBM.

Patience is in short supply in this era of instant gratification. Youngsters today are more concerned with cash in hand than what they will receive after 10-20 years. They do not think of long-term benefits and give no significance to benefits such as gratuity.

This can be a costly error in judgment. Even with a small increase in your basic salary, your gratuity corpus can become extremely large in the long-term. If someone starts his career at a basic salary of ₹ 30,000 and gets a nominal 10% increment every year, his gratuity at the end of 20 years will be ₹ 14.1 lacs. However, the Payment of Gratuity Act, 1972, places a cap of ₹ 10 lacs on the amount that a company has to pay as gratuity, although a company is free to give more if it wants to.

In addition, the tax exemption limit for gratuity has now been raised to ₹ 10 lacs, which makes this long-term benefit even more attractive. "You should consider the fact that a lump sum of up to ₹ 10 lacs you get is tax-free while the raise in your next salary would be taxable. So when you decide to change jobs and there are only a few months left for entitlement of the gratuity, buy some more time from the new employer so that you are able to avail this benefit," says Veer Sardesai, a Pune-based certified financial planner.

Governed by the Payment of Gratuity Act, 1972, gratuity is a defined benefit plan. It is mandatory for companies with more than 10 employees on their payrolls to give gratuity to an employee on resignation, retirement and termination of service. However, an employee is eligible for this benefit only on completion of five years of continuous service with the company.

Financial Investment Tools

Bank Fixed Deposits (FDs)	Stocks
Bank Recurring Deposits (RDs)	Bonds
PPF (Public Provident Fund)	Mutual Funds
EPF (Employee Provident Fund)	FMPs (Fixed Maturity Plans) of MFs
VPF (Voluntary Provident Fund)	Commodities
Gratuity	Life Insurance
Superannuation	Real Estate
Gold	

Superannuation

A superannuation fund is one of the other retirement benefits given to employees by a company. The company pays 15% of basic wages as a contribution to superannuation[54]. There is no contribution from the employee.

Normally the company has a link with agencies like LIC

Superannuation Fund, where their contributions are paid. This contribution is invested by the fund in various securities as per a prescribed investment pattern. Interest on contributions is credited to the members' account. Normally the rate of interest is equivalent to the PF interest rate.

On attaining retirement age, a member is eligible to take 25% of the balance available in his/her account as a tax free benefit. The balance 75% is put into an annuity fund, and the agency (LIC) will pay the member monthly/quarterly/periodic annuity returns depending on the option exercised by the member. This payment, received regularly, is taxable.

In case an employee resigns, the employee has the option to transfer the amount to the new employer. If the new employer does not have a superannuation scheme, then the employee can withdraw the amount in the account, subject to deduction of tax and approval of the IT department, or retain the amount in the fund, till the superannuation age (58 years).

Retirement benefits

All the retirement benefit plans described in the last few sections of this book, whether EPF, VPF, gratuity or superannuation, seem like simple and traditional ways to block your money. The fact remains that these benefits are hardly understood by today's generation.

To me, they are an excellent source of wealth accumulation for beginners on to the journey to financial freedom. Not only do they force you to put some money into a corpus every month, they discourage you to break the benefits that compounding money has to offer you.

This is an ideal start up strategy for any one new in this journey.

As you see your money grow and as you see the benefits of compounding, you are likely to realize that the goal of financial freedom is a reality, and it can be achieved by commitment, dedication, discipline and perseverance.

I want to narrate an incident in my life that lead me to realize the power of compound interest. I had gone to the State Bank of India to have my PPF passbook updated. In those days accounts like PPF were not available online and you had to physically go to the bank to perform any transactions or to even get your passbook updated.

As I was about to leave for the bank, my father gave me the PPF pass book of my eldest brother so that I could have it updated too. I went to the bank and got both the pass books updated. While driving back home, I just glanced through both the pass books just to make sure that the pass book updates reflected all transactions to date. I was astounded to see that my brother was earning lacs of rupees as yearly interest on the money he was holding in the bank, and that these lacs of rupees of interest would further pay him multiples of lacs next year because they would be added to the principal amount next year and he would earn interest on the interest as it keeps compounding. (We will talk more about the power of compounding in the later sections of the book.)

This incident made a deep impact on me and my way of thinking about these traditional investment methodologies. Many questions crossed my mind at that moment:

How can people earn lacs of rupees in interest when I am struggling to deposit ₹ 50,000 in the account every year?

Are they earning so much more than what I am earning?

Am I missing something in this concept of wealth generation?

Was there something I didn't know, and if so what was it?

Sooner rather than later, I realized the power of compounding and the role that it plays in wealth generation and financial freedom. Now, when I see my EPF and PPF statements every year and see the interest earned in that year, I feel powerful. I can actually feel it. You have to experience it to realize how big this can get.

As I said earlier, just these retirement benefits alone are enough to make you a millionaire. They are a very important part of your portfolio. You just have to be disciplined, have patience and commit yourself and be commited.

Let us now move to relatively lesser known investment vehicles. There are some very important investment tools listed here, some of which you will definitely need to make sure you stay ahead of inflation.

Financial Investment Tools	
Bank Fixed Deposits (FDs)	Stocks
Bank Recurring Deposits (RDs)	Bonds
PPF (Public Provident Fund)	Mutual Funds
EPF (Employee Provident Fund)	FMPs (Fixed Maturity Plans) of MFs
VPF (Voluntary Provident Fund)	Commodities
Gratuity	Life Insurance
Superannuation	Real Estate
Gold	

Gold

Having seen most of the traditional investment vehicles, let us look at gold as an investment vehicle. In India, and in many other countries, gold is just seen as a security in case of an emergency or in case of important occasions in life such as marriage. Traditionally, we never think of gold as an investment vehicle and a way to help us reach financial success. This may be because of the culture that we have been brought up in.

However, things are changing. Today's generation is using gold as an important element in their portfolio investments. As an investment, you expect gold to beat inflation and give returns which you can use elsewhere. It is no longer a dead investment like jewellery, that lies in your bank locker and for which you pay charges.

Today, gold is assumed to be an excellent diversification in your portfolio. In fact, no portfolio can be said to be complete without a defined and planned element of gold investment. It is not only an excellent hedge against inflation but also the best bet in the event of a big risk that you are otherwise carrying in your portfolio.

Gold should be an important part of a diversified investment portfolio because its price increases in response to events that cause the value of paper investments, such as stocks and bonds, to decline. This is important to understand. Those of you who have invested actively in stocks will have realized the inverse relationship between gold and the stock market. So, when you know that markets are doing well, it is time to start taking out money at a handsome profit and invest it in gold, because gold would typically go down at that stage. The opposite is also true.

When the markets drop, investors typically lose trust in stocks and economies of the world and turn back to the most trusted and traditional investment i.e., gold. You will learn about this in more detail and why it happens in later sections of the book. However, the important thing to keep in mind is that once you have learnt about this relationship between gold, stock prices and the health of the economy in general, you can use this knowledge to your advantage.

Although the price of gold can be volatile in the short-term, it has always maintained its value in the long-term. Over the years, it has served as a hedge against inflation and the erosion of major currencies, and thus is an investment well worth considering.

Figure 11 represents the returns from gold vs the returns from stocks during specific crisis triggers across the world. This should give you a fair idea on the importance of gold as a strong part of your portfolio. The returns from gold have, more or less, always been consistent irrespective of any market crises that may have occurred in the last two decades.

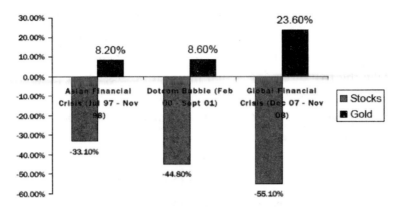

Fig 11: *Gold vs stocks*

Another interesting statistics is to look at is the returns from gold over the last few decades. Figure 12 shows that over the last 19 years, gold has grown at an annualized rate of 11%, while annualized inflation has been less than 6%. This makes it clearly evident that gold is an excellent hedge against event risk as well as against inflation.

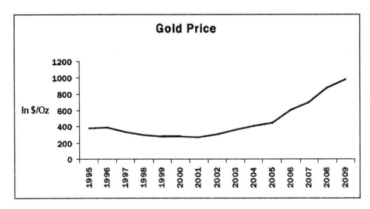

Fig 12: *Returns from gold in the last two decades*

Traditionally, keeping the gold safe has been the biggest obstacle to making large investments using this investment vehicle.

Things have changed and evolved with time. Nowadays, it is very easy to invest in gold with the availability of gold Exchange Traded Funds[55] (ETFs). Gone are the days when you needed to take the risk of having actual physical possession of gold and worrying about re-selling the same at an appropriate time at the right price. Gold ETFs open up a completely new and flexible investment option.

Gold ETFs

Gold Exchange Traded Funds (ETFs) are intended to offer investors a means of participating in the gold bullion market[56] without the necessity of taking physical delivery of gold. In other words, investing in gold ETFs is investing in gold in dematerialized[57] (demat) form.

Gold ETFs are designed to provide returns that closely correspond to the returns provided by physical gold. Each ETF unit is approximately equal to the price of 1 gm of gold (or may be 10 grams of gold in some ETFs).

Some of the clear merits of investing in gold ETFs over traditional investment techniques are as follows:

1. They are potentially cheaper as compared to other available avenues, like jewellery. In the latter, there is too much overhead in the cutting, polishing and other labour costs. These do not apply to gold ETFs.

2. It is quick and convenient to deal through your demat account. You do have to go to the bank or the jeweller to buy or sell gold. It is as easy as buying or selling any other stock that you have. You can buy and sell at will.

3. There are no storage or security issues. Since you do not possess any physical gold, you eliminate all the risks associated with the upkeep of the same.

4. The pricing is transparent. The same prices are available to everybody. You do not have to worry about the price of the gold or its purity.

5. Gold ETFs are listed and traded just like any other stock. You can buy or sell them through demat and trading online account or through the stock broker that you normally deal with for transaction of your other stocks. So, you do not need any additional setup to start investing in gold ETFs.

6. They are ideal for a retail investor as the minimum size is 1 unit. This is the real booster for beginners and retail investors who want to make systematic monthly investments in gold. Imagine how difficult it would be to go to a jeweller and buy 1 gm of gold every month.

Overall, gold ETFs are the best avenue from an investment perspective as compared to other gold investment avenues.

Figure 13 shows a comparative analysis and the advantages that gold ETFs clearly have over all other gold investment avenues.

Transaction Charges	Jewellery	Gold Bars	Gold ETF
Purchase	Making charges of 15-20%	10% to 20% mark-up charges by banks.	Brokerage of 0.5% or even less.
Sell	10% - 20% is lost due to Purity issues	Banks do not take it back, so premium paid at time of purchase is written off.	Brokerage of 0.5% or even less.
Maintenance	Insurance charges and locker charges (if you put it in locker)	Insurance charges and locker charges (if you put it in locker)	1.00%
Tax Implications	Long-term capital gain, but after 3 years, plus wealth tax	Long-term capital gain, but after 3 years, plus wealth tax	Long-term Capital tax of, but after 1 year. No wealth tax

Fig 13: *Gold ETFs vs other gold investment avenues*

How much you should invest in gold depends on the risk reward weightage that you want to give gold. A balanced portfolio should have anywhere between 5 to 10% of the money invested in gold.

Once you are a mature investor, these percentage allocations of various investments in your portfolio, including that of gold, can keep changing depending on the environmental factors and how the market is behaving.

I have personally moved up to 8% of portfolio investments in gold and even came down to 0% when I thought that gold had reached its peak, and I should be investing in stocks or even relatively longer term fixed deposits because they were offering extremely high returns at some stage. I may again push some of my investments in gold if I see a potential for gold prices to rise faster than stock prices or fixed deposits.

If you are a start up investor, make a Systematic Investment Plan (SIP) to invest small amounts regularly in gold and build up a significant worth. Keep a watch on the market trends in stocks and gold on a daily or at least a weekly basis to see how these prices fluctuate and how they are also related to each other. A stage will come when you will be able to make informed judgments around these price fluctuations and will be confident of taking independent decisions about how to vary your portfolio allocation to maximize your returns. Remember that this will not only take time but also a lot of hard work and commitment.

Which decisions in the global economy impact stocks and gold and in what way? Why does this happen? Find the answers to these questions. There is no short cut. It took me almost seven years to understand all these concepts before I started moving the investments around in my portfolio to maximize returns.

Financial Investment Tools	
Bank Fixed Deposits (FDs)	Stocks
Bank Recurring Deposits (RDs)	Bonds
PPF (Public Provident Fund)	Mutual Funds
EPF (Employee Provident Fund)	FMPs (Fixed Maturity Plans) of MFs
VPF (Voluntary Provident Fund)	Commodities
Gratuity	Life Insurance
Superannuation	Real Estate
Gold	

Stocks

As Warren Buffet, the world's most famous billionaire investor once said:

"Most people get interested in stocks when everyone else is. The time to get interested is when no one else is. You can't buy what is popular and do well."

This is one area of investment where I have seen people shying away saying it is too risky to invest in stocks. On the other hand I have seen even my close relatives borrow money and invest everything they had in stocks while some families have been wiped out financially, even having to sell their houses, because they lost everything in the stock market.

I have always believed in an old saying "knowledge removes fear". Since the topic itself is so sensitive, let us first try and gain some awareness about stocks. Even if you never buy a single stock but invest in bonds and mutual funds, you still need to have a good understanding of how the stock market works. In the long run however, stock prices usually reflect the growth (or decline) of any company's earnings.

Let us start with a very simple example.

Suppose that instead of asking you for a loan, your brother invites you to invest in his latest business idea – creating energy from city waste. You bought 100 shares of his company by paying ₹ 10 per share. The business takes off and the company announces that it will pay all shareholders an annual dividend of 60 paisa per share, i.e., 6% returns on your investment.

Suppose that ten years later Suzlon Energy wants to buy your brother's company and are ready to pay ₹ 100 per share. So, your realized capital gains are around 900% in 10 years.

Hence, you earned both the cash flow through dividends as well as the capital gains on your smart investment. We will study these concepts in the following sections.

What is a share of stock?

When a company wants to grow faster than its current earnings and profits would allow it to grow, it looks for additional sources of capital for expansion. This capital can be in the form of a "debt" capital or an "equity" capital.

For a debt[58] capital, the company would normally approach a bank or any other finance company to obtain a loan. Once it acquires a loan, it can invest the money in its business, earn more money and return the loan amount with interest. The bank or the financial institution, in such a case, is not interested in being a part of the company and is only interested in getting its principal back with a fixed interest.

For an equity[59] capital, the company would have to approach the public to invest money in the company and in return take an "equity" stake in the company. The company can approach the public through multiple means as explained.

IPO

There is a limit to how much a company can borrow in the form of a bank loan. Too much debt can saddle a company as it has to pay back large interest payments through its current earnings till the new earnings start bearing results. Often, this is not feasible because of the large gestation periods involved in most businesses before the company starts actually earning on the investments made.

What if a company cannot afford so much debt and still wants to go ahead and expand? In this case, the company will seek "equity capital" instead of "debt capital". Equity capital is not required to be paid back. All a company has to do in exchange for equity capital is give part ownership of the company. That is the company goes "public" and floats an Initial Public Offering[60] (IPO).

To float an IPO, the price per share and the number of shares to be sold are determined jointly by the company and the investment banker. A public offering is the only time investors can buy stock directly from the company. At all other times, investors buy and sell shares from each other via a stock exchange[61] like the Bombay Stock Exchange (BSE) and the National Stock Exchange(NSE).

Price of a share and fluctuations

What determines the price of the stock is essentially the number of buy or sell orders for that stock. If the ratio of buy and sell orders is even, then the stock will continue to trade at the same price.

If the number of buy orders is higher than the sell orders (which means that the company that has issued the shares is doing well and everyone wants to hold its shares), then it will trade at a higher price.

On the other side, if there are more sell orders than buy orders (which means that the share issuing company is not performing well and no one wants to hold shares in such a company), then it will trade at a lower price.

The above fluctuations in share prices are very logical and mathematical. Let us say that a company floats an IPO issue distributing 1000 shares at ₹ 10 per share. The total price of stock is ₹ 10,000. Suppose the company is doing well and many people want to buy shares of this company. If 200 more people want to buy this stock at ₹ 10, then the total additional amount that will be invested is Rs.2000. The total number of shares does not change, as each share represents a holding in the company. Thus the total amount available is now ₹ 12,000 for the same number (1000) of shares. If these 'buy' orders are executed (which means there is a seller for those shares), the price of one share obviously becomes ₹ 12 (up from ₹ 10). The same holds true when sell orders are executed.

When the price of the stock becomes too high, the company will occasionally decide to split the price of the stock to encourage trading liquidity.

As a long-term investor, you should not be too concerned with frequent fluctuations in share prices if you are sure that the company is earning well, making good profits and has strong fundamentals. Temporary fluctuations can occur because of innumerable and uncontrollable market factors.

Moreover, if you have invested for cash flow, then it actually does not matter if there are temporary fluctuations as long as the company is earning well.

P/E ratio

The P/E ratio[62] or the Price vs Earning ratio is essentially the ratio of the price per share vs the earning per share of the company. Earnings Per Share[63] are also termed as EPS. Generally, the higher the P/E ratio, the more expensive is the stock. Expensive stock means that the price is already high and we should be careful when investing in such a stock. P/E ratios are useful for comparison of companies in the same industry. If the average P/E ratio of most of the companies in a particular industry is around 18 and the company you are interested in investing in has a P/E ratio of around 21, it essentially means that the said stock is expensive and the market is expecting the company to have significantly higher earnings and has already built in the expectations in the stock price. This does not mean that the said stock is a bad investment; it only tells that you can go ahead and invest but you are paying a premium price to do so.

A P/E ratio of 21 essentially means that the price per share is 21 times the earnings per share.

Remember that a stock's P/E ratio is just one of the factors (though a very important one) which can help you guide on a buying decision.

Dividends

"Dividends" are an extremely important aspect of stocks that can give you a very good incoming cash flow. If you have planned well and want more assured returns, invest for dividends rather than to increase the stock value of the company.

Dividends[64] are the returns you get as a share holder of the company in which you are a partial owner. Dividends are paid out of earnings, unless the company ploughs all the earnings back into the company to fuel future growth.

Whenever a company earns a profit, it distributes part of the profit as dividend to stock holders. The amount of dividend paid out by the company is best measured by the dividend payout ratio[65], which is defined as the ratio of dividend distributed by the company to the Total Profit earned after Tax[66] (PAT). If a company has a dividend payout ratio of over 50% it means that the company is distributing 50% of the earnings back to its shareholders and may be investing the remaining 50% to fuel future growth. Such companies with a dividend payout ratio of 50% or more are distributing the dividend generously.

However, there is an alternative way of measuring how much dividend you get on a stock — called the dividend yield[67]. This is the amount of dividend you get per stock divided by the price you pay. Note that dividend yield changes as the price of the stock changes. The dividend yield of a stock can be high, either because the company has a high dividend payout ratio, or simply because its stock price is very low.

In any case, if what matters to you is the dividend you get for your money invested, you should look at the dividend yield. In exceptional cases when the dividend yield is low because of the poor earnings of the company (due to some known environmental factors) but the dividend payout ratio is still high, it essentially means that the company is still distributing a good percentage of its earnings. In such a case the stock may still be a good investment from the perspective of cash flow, from the dividends.

Dividends are tax-free income for the shareholders. They are far more profitable today than they were in the last four years. In fact, a dividend yield of 6.5% is equivalent to 10% interest earned through a fixed deposit or any other debt based investment, over a period of one year, which is taxable income. In fact, in western countries, a large number of people invest solely for dividends.

The clear advantages of income from dividends over traditional and inefficient mechanism like fixed deposits, are given below.

1. Gives you a fixed regular income.

2. The income earned through dividends is completely tax free since the company has already paid taxes while

calculating the PAT and you are receiving the dividend as a shareholder of the company.

3. Also, while you are enjoying the dividend, the capital value of the stocks that you are holding is also likely to give you good results since these stocks belong to typically stable blue chip stocks.

4. The dividend in high dividend stocks also acts as a safety cushion that prevents the script from a free fall. The reason is very simple. As you are aware, stock prices go down only if there are more sellers than buyers for that specific stock. For high dividend performing stocks, investors are wary of losing the regular dividend cash inflow if they sell too much, thus avoiding a free fall.

5. This cycle typically results in high dividend stocks yielding high capital gains as well. In other words, companies that boost their dividend payment are also likely to outperform the stocks that pay contracting dividends.

There are four important dates to remember regarding dividends.

Declaration date: The declaration date is the day the Board of Directors announce their intention to pay a dividend. On this day, the company creates a liability on its books; it now owes the money to the stockholders. On the declaration date, the board will also announce a date of record date and a payment date.

Date of record: The date of record is the date on which a company reviews its records to determine exactly who its shareholders are - an investor must be a "holder of record" in order to receive a dividend payout. A stock will almost always begin trading ex-dividend (or "ex-rights") the second business day before the record date.

Ex-dividend date: The ex-dividend date of a stock is the single most important date for dividend investors to consider. To receive a stock's upcoming dividend, an investor must purchase shares of the stock prior to the ex-dividend date. This also means he can sell a stock on the ex-dividend date and still receive the dividends even though shares have not yet been placed in his account.

Payment date: This is the date the dividend will actually be given to the shareholders of company.

The importance of dividend payout will be clear, from Figure 14, which depicts the price performance of two groups between 31 March 2009 and 29 July 2011.

In the first group, the stock prices of companies that had increased the dividend payment appreciated by 286% on an average. The share prices in the second group, which included companies with falling or stagnant dividends, had risen by 129% on an average. During the same period, the Sensex, which also included companies that had not paid any dividends, rose by 87.44%. All these returns are in absolute terms.

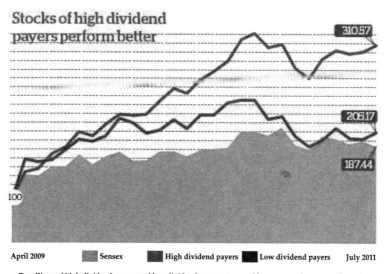

Stocks of high dividend payers perform better

310.57

206.17

187.44

100

April 2009 ▇ Sensex ▇ High dividend payers ▇ Low dividend payers July 2011

Trendlines of high dividend payers and low dividend payers are monthly average prices across the various companies in their respective groups. Both the groups and the Sensex are normalised to a base of 100.

Fig 14: *Analysis of high and low dividend stocks*

The analysis in Fig 14 underlines the market's perception of dividend payout. Both groups contained dividend paying stocks, but the first group generated more than twice the returns delivered by the second group. Also, both managed to outperform the broader market. Whether they increase or decrease the dividend payout, the stocks that give a regular income will be able to outperform the general market substantially. If you have done enough research, you can always find good stocks to invest in, which not only assure very good dividends but also can help you realize capital gains in case you need to at some date.

Experts like Robert Kiyosaki believe that we should never sell either real estate or stocks because they are the source of incoming cash flows. If you have invested enough for incoming cash flows, you will do quite well even in challenging economic times and market conditions. This is also evident from the graphs in Fig 14.

Some of the stocks that I have been monitoring and investing in, that yield good dividends are mentioned overleaf:

- Hindustan Unilever (HUL)
- Tata Tea
- SRF
- NIIT Tech
- L&T
- GAIL
- EIL
- GE Shipping
- ONGC
- ITC
- IOCL
- NTPC

While there are distinct advantages of stocks that yield good dividends, it must be noted, at this stage, that mature companies with high dividend yields usually have a very stable stock price and therefore limited upside potential. Since a good part of the earnings are distributed as dividends, the company can plough back less earnings into expansion of its business. Hence it is likely to have a limited upside potential.

To conclude, while deciding which stocks to invest in based on the cash flow guidelines, you should look for mature companies that yield high dividends. If you are looking for more capital gains rather than cash flow, you should look for stocks which may not provide high dividends but have more growth potential (and are investing their earnings in growth).

A mature investor will typically invest for cash flow and only when they have enough wealth, will they want to take certain risks with companies that yield low dividends, but have high growth potential.

What is a demat account?

A *demat* account[68] is short for "dematerialized account" i.e., holding shares in an electronic form rather than in a physical form (paper). The electronic holdings are reflected in an online account usually held with a Depository Participant[69] (DP), which is an institution authorized by a depository to act on its behalf. A DP could also be an authorized bank.

A demat account is a safe and convenient means of holding securities[70] just as a bank account is safe and convenient for funds. Today, practically 99.9% settlement (of shares) takes place in the demat mode only.

Figure 15, shows a comparison of the functioning of a demat account against a normal bank account, which will help you to understand a demat account better.

No.	Basis Of Differentiation	Bank Account	Demat Account
1	Form of Holdings/Deposits	Funds	Securities
2	Used for	Safekeeping of money	Safekeeping of shares
3	Facilitates	Transfer of money (without actually handling Transfer of shares (without actually handling money)	Transfer of shares (without actually handling shares)
4	Where to open	A bank of choice	A DP of choice (can be a bank)
5	Requirement of PAN Number	Not Mandatory	Mandatory (effective from April 01, 2006)
6	Interest accrual on holdings	Interest income is subject to the applicable rate of interest	No interest accruals on securities held in demat account

No.	Basis Of Differentiation	Bank Account	Demat Account
7	Minimum balance requirement	AQB* maintenance is specified for certain bank accounts	No such requirement
8	Either or Survivor facility	Available	Not available

Fig 15: *Comparison of a demat account vs a bank account*

How to open a demat account

You will need a demat account whether you want to invest in gold ETFs, running equities or IPOs.

To start dealing in any kind of securities in electronic form, you need to open a demat account with a DP of your choice. If you already have shares in the physical form you should ensure the account is opened under the same set of names that appear on the share certificate; otherwise a new account can be opened in any desired pattern by the investor.

Firstly, choose a DP. I chose HDFC Securities but you could approach any other DP like ICICI Direct, Share Khan, India Bulls, Reliance Money.

To open an account you have to fill up the form provided by the DP, and sign an agreement with the DP in a standard format prescribed by the depository.

The DP provides the investor with a copy of the agreement and schedule of charges for future reference. It is important to note the brokerage charges that will be deducted from each securities transaction conducted through your demat account. Normally, it should be around 0.25% or less. The brokerage charge may sound insignificant in the beginning but will become quite large as you proceed on your journey towards financial freedom, since the number and amount of transactions will grow in your equity part of the portfolio.

It would be wise to make sure that you have chosen a reliable DP even if the brokerage is slightly on the higher side.

A DP opens the account and provides you with a unique account number through which you will be able to transact your securities through secured internet sites as well as over the telephone.

Advantages of demat account

A demat account in electronic form is definitely better as compared to the traditional way of dealing with shares manually. Some of the advantages of a demat account are given below.

▶ It is a safe and convenient way of holding securities (equity and debt instruments both).

▶ Transactions involving physical securities are costlier than those involving dematerialized securities (just like the transactions through a bank teller are costlier than ATM transactions). Therefore, the charges applicable to an investor are less for each transaction.

▶ Securities can be transferred immediately an instruction is given.

▶ It gives increased liquidity, as securities can be sold at any time during the day trading hours, and payment can be received in a very short period of time.

▶ There are no stamp duty charges.

▶ Risks like forgery, thefts, bad delivery, delays in transfer etc., associated with physical certificates, are eliminated.

▶ Securities can be pledged in a short period of time.

▶ Paper work and transaction costs are reduced.

- Odd-lot shares can also be traded (even 1 share).

- Nomination facility is available.

- Any change in address or bank account details can be electronically intimated to all companies in which an investor holds any securities, without having to inform each of them separately.

- Securities are transferred by the DP itself, so there is no need to correspond with the individual companies.

- Shares arising out of bonus, splits, consolidation, mergers etc., are automatically credited into the demat account of the investor.

- Shares allotted in public issues are directly credited into the demat account of the applicant, very quickly.

Financial Investment Tools	
Bank Fixed Deposits (FDs)	Stocks
Bank Recurring Deposits (RDs)	Bonds
PPF (Public Provident Fund)	Mutual Funds
EPF (Employee Provident Fund)	FMPs (Fixed Maturity Plans) of MFs
VPF (Voluntary Provident Fund)	Commodities
Gratuity	Life Insurance
Superannuation	Real Estate
Gold	

Bonds

While stocks are unpredictable and carry an element of risk with them, bonds[71] tell you how much income you will receive during the life of the bond.

As mentioned earlier in the section on stocks, a company looking to expand and needing money can go in for raising debt capital or equity capital. Equity investments make you an owner of the company while debt investments in the company make you a loaner. When someone invests in debt capital, he or she is investing his or her money as loan (in effect) and is therefore termed as a "loaner."

A company may seek debt capital in the same manner as equity capital from the public. To get debt capital from the public (with fixed interest and tenure), the company contacts an investment banker who arranges for debt securities, called bonds to be sold to the public. These bonds are purchased by investors who are interested in earning a fixed interest in a fixed tenure. Often, governments and state municipalities also issue bonds to raise debt capital.

The main factor in bonds is the interest rate charged by the bank. If the borrower's credit rating[72] is low, the bank will charge a higher interest rate to compensate for the additional risk.

How bonds trade

Bonds trade in the open market, just like stocks. If you buy bonds with the intention of keeping them till maturity, then you may not be concerned how bonds trade in the market place. But if you intend to sell bonds before the maturity period, it is better to understand how bond trading takes place.

Let us say that after 6 months of purchasing the bond, the interest rates go up in the market, for some reason. If you have to sell your bond in the market under such circumstances, you would have to obviously bring the price of the bond down to cover for the lower interest rate that you are getting on your bond (which was fixed at the time of purchase of the bond) as compared to the market interest rate. The reasoning is the same if the interest rates in the market go down.

Are bonds safer than stocks?

Bonds have been traditionally assumed to be safer than stocks. But if there is a chance that you may have to sell them before the maturity period, the interest rate can vary a lot depending on the market conditions.

Unlike bank fixed deposits, current market interest rates govern the price of a bond when you try to sell it, unless you sell it only when it matures. The most important thing to remember about bonds is that when interest rates go up, bond prices go down and vice versa.

One must also be sure of the credit rating of the company that has issued the bond. This can be found through credit advisors[73] or credit rating agencies[73] like S&P, Moody's etc. Bond prices may also plummet if the credit rating of a specific bond goes down with time. The opposite is true if the credit rating goes up.

When should you invest in bonds?

There are a number of reasons why many people prefer bonds during specific times in the market. Some of them are:

1. If you have a good feel for interest rates and are aware that the interest rates are near their peak and ready to

drop, you should obviously buy bonds at the current fixed high interest rates.

2. By themselves, bonds may not offer too much, but combined with other stock investments, they can give balance to a portfolio.

3. The government often issues tax free bonds for the public to invest in. Tax saving can be a trigger to enter the bond market. I have purchased infrastructure bonds, issued by the Indian government, for the construction of flyovers and general infrastructure. These not only provided tax free returns but gave me the opportunity to contribute my money towards the nation's infrastructure development. Typically, the tax rebates offered by such bonds are over and above the traditional tax rebates normally offered under Section 80C etc. As was the case with most people, I did not sell the bonds in the open market but retained them as fixed tenure, fixed interest rate investment tools till maturity.

To conclude, we can consider bonds as an investment between fixed deposits and stock. They give you the flexibility of selling them before they mature, just as you can sell a stock (may be at a higher price, if the interest rate is more than the interest rate at which you purchased them).

At the same time, they are a low risk investment, like any fixed interest, fixed tenure investment, such as fixed deposit.

Over and above this flexibility, they can help you save taxes as well. Considering all this, bonds are an important part of the debt portion of the portfolio. How much should you invest in bonds depends on the risk and reward ratio with which you are building your portfolio and the breakup of debt and equity that you are looking at. Your age, country, risk taking capability and other environmental factors play a pivotal role in deciding the distribution of your portfolio.

Financial Investment Tools	
Bank Fixed Deposits (FDs)	Stocks
Bank Recurring Deposits (RDs)	Bonds
PPF (Public Provident Fund)	**Mutual Funds**
EPF (Employee Provident Fund)	FMPs (Fixed Maturity Plans) of MFs
VPF (Voluntary Provident Fund)	Commodities
Gratuity	Life Insurance
Superannuation	Real Estate
Gold	

Mutual Funds

Mutual funds[74] are a very popular investment vehicle because they allow you to invest in stocks and bonds without having the stress of deciding the right ones to buy or the right time to sell.

When you invest in mutual funds, it goes into a pool of money along with other peoples investments. The portfolio manager starts investing the collected money into various stocks and bonds in the market. The mutual fund company issues shares to the investors so that they have an ownership in the fund.

As the investment grows, the Net Asset Value (NAV) [75] or the price per share of the fund goes up (since the number of shares is fixed at the time of launch of the mutual fund scheme) and so do your likely returns. As with stock, you can track the NAV of your mutual fund at the end of every day. While the stock prices are calculated at real time, the NAV of a mutual fund scheme is calculated at the end of every day based on the investments accumulated at the end of the day.

When you buy mutual funds (or shares in a mutual fund to be precise), you do not know the exact composition of the stocks or bonds where the money has been invested or will be invested in future. You are going to primarily trust the portfolio manager[76] assigned to the mutual fund scheme to do the job he has been hired to do.

How mutual funds make money

Just as we make money out of stocks, mutual funds generate money in two ways:

1. Through capital gains – Buy low and sell high

2. Through cash flow – Income from securities in the portfolio i.e., dividends in the case of stocks and interest payments in the case of bonds.

Why you should invest in mutual funds

There are distinct advantages in holding mutual fund portfolios. Some of the salient ones are listed below:

1. They allow you to hold an extremely diversified portfolio at a very small investment. You might have a portfolio of the best 50 companies in the market with an investment of ₹ 500.

2. Portfolios are professionally managed, so you do not have to worry about picking up the right securities at the right time and selling them at an appropriate time.

Some demerits of mutual funds

While mutual funds have their own distinct advantages over stocks, they have certain demerits as well.

1. Every time you buy shares in a mutual fund, they charge entry fees, which can be very high in some cases. This fee essentially is for the portfolio manager and his team to manage the fund.

2. Funds also incur operating costs to keep the fund running.

All fees incurred are mentioned in the prospectus of the mutual fund and should be considered while selecting which mutual fund to invest in, from the thousands of choices you have today.

Some of the mutual funds that I have invested in are:

1. Reliance Pharma Fund – Growth plan

2. Reliance Regular Savings Fund – Equity plan – Growth option

3. UTI Pharma and Healthcare Fund

All mutual fund transactions whether buying more funds, selling funds, or generating your transaction statements for any given period can be done online and do not require you to run around filling forms and making physical deposits.

Financial Investment Tools	
Bank Fixed Deposits (FDs)	Stocks
Bank Recurring Deposits (RDs)	Bonds
PPF (Public Provident Fund)	Mutual Funds
EPF (Employee Provident Fund)	**FMPs (Fixed Maturity Plans) of MFs**
VPF (Voluntary Provident Fund)	Commodities
Gratuity	Life Insurance
Superannuation	Real Estate
Gold	

FMPs (Fixed Maturity Plans) of MFs

Whenever inflation figures are on the rise, the interest rates offered by banks on deposits also start rising. This may look like a rosy picture for those who derive a major chunk of their income from fixed deposits as banks now offer more interest for the same amount, but what about the fixed deposits made earlier?

Has the interest offered by banks on these deposits also increased? The simple answer is "no" – the interest offered by banks has increased only for the new deposits.

Again, what happens if tomorrow, the banks increase their interest rates? Will they offer a higher interest on the FDs that you have made today? The answer, again, is "no".

With the answer to both the above questions being 'no', what can you as a retail investor do? You prefer not to invest in the stock market to avoid the hassles of timing the market. But again, in the fixed income products as well, you have to time the market!

With the manner and the speed at which the interest rates fluctuate these days, timing the market has become an important criterion for investing in fixed income instruments as well. Therefore, you will need a professional team who understands these fluctuations and can time the market for you.

Just as mutual funds employ professionally qualified staff to invest in the stock markets on behalf of the retail investors, there are fixed income products which have professionally qualified staff for investing in fixed income securities.

Fixed Maturity Plans (FMPs) [77] are close ended[78] mutual fund debt schemes that have a predetermined maturity date. They predominantly invest in government securities, corporate debt, commercial papers and money market instruments and aim at generating steady returns over a fixed period. They protect the investors against market fluctuations by investing in securities in line with their maturity periods.

The maturity period of the FMP varies from one plan to another. Unlike other debt funds, an investor can opt for a maturity period that suits his needs best. Depending on the tenure of the FMP, the fund manager invests in a combination of the above mentioned instruments of similar maturity. For example, if the FMP is for a year, then the fund manager invests in paper maturing in one year.

FMPs are close-ended in nature which means that once the New Fund Offer (NFO) closes, the scheme cannot accept any further investment.

FMPs offer you most of the advantages that mutual funds offer, such as diversified investment, professional management. The risks are obviously lower since these plans do not invest in stocks. FMPs are an upcoming trend and it is worth trying out a small investment of your debt portfolio with FMPs and see if the professionals can manage the debt part of the portfolio better than you personally can. If you are tight on bandwidth, this of course is a good choice.

I have personally invested in FMPs recently, with a two year block in period and am hopeful of getting better results than what I get through fixed deposits. In conclusion, I would like to say that FMPs are a good low risk debt part of your portfolio.

Financial Investment Tools	
Bank Fixed Deposits (FDs)	Stocks
Bank Recurring Deposits (RDs)	Bonds
PPF (Public Provident Fund)	Mutual Funds
EPF (Employee Provident Fund)	FMPs (Fixed Maturity Plans) of MFs
VPF (Voluntary Provident Fund)	**Commodities**
Gratuity	Life Insurance
Superannuation	Real Estate
Gold	

Commodities

Trading volumes in the commodities[79] market are picking up in India as the volatility and attractiveness of returns draws more and more investors. Investment in commodities can be made by day traders as well as medium- to long-term position investors. Commodities are being used by global investors for hedging and hence are a good investment option for position investors.

Trading in commodities is especially attractive due to the higher risk/return ratio. Commodities trades are highly leveraged, which means that the margin requirement for trading in commodities futures is quite low in comparison to overall position holding.

Therefore, it magnifies the gains and losses of an investor. Commodities prices are seeing a lot of volatility in the recent times. The price fluctuation is due to turbulence in global markets, monsoon, demand-supply mismatch and high liquidity.

Some of the major categories traded in the markets, their outlook and ways an investor can invest in them are given below.

Industrial metals

Industrial commodities include aluminium, copper, nickel, zinc, steel, etc. The price movement of industrial commodities depends on the macro-economic factors in the world economy, for example, financial turbulence in China, border tensions in Korea, etc. These commodities do well when investors are confident about consumption demand from large economies like China. Investors can invest in industrial commodities by taking speculative future positions through a commodities broker or investing in commodities-based stocks. Though there is no one-to-one co-relation between commodity prices and commodities stock price movement, if all other things are equal, commodity prices form the most important factor in the pricing of commodities-based stocks.

Precious metals

This category includes precious metals like gold, silver and platinum. Gold and silver are trading at all-time high levels and experts believe there is room for further appreciation in the medium term. Investment appetite in precious metals has gone up tremendously in recent years due to global economic uncertainties. Large global investors as well as central banks in some countries are investing in precious metals to hedge against global economic uncertainties.

Gold

Gold is one of the most important precious metal commodity items that is traded in the open market. Because of its importance and the sheer number of transactions, it has been covered as a separate section already in the book.

Gold is unique for its durability (it does not rust or otherwise corrode), malleability and its ability to conduct both heat and electricity. It has some industrial applications in dentistry and electronics, but we know it principally as a base for jewellery and as a form of currency.

The value of gold is determined by the market 24 hours a day, nearly seven days a week. Gold trades predominantly as a function of sentiment; its price is less affected by the laws of supply and demand. This is because new mine supply is vastly outweighed by the sheer size of above-ground — hoarded gold.

Several factors account for an increased desire to hoard the yellow metal:

1. **Systemic financial concerns**

    When banks and money are perceived as unstable or political stability is questionable, gold has often been sought as a safe store of value.

2. **Inflation**

    When real rates of return in the equity, bond or real estate markets are negative, people regularly flock to gold as an asset that will maintain its value.

3. **War or political crises**

    War and political upheaval have always sent people into a gold-hoarding mode. An entire lifetime's worth of savings can be made portable and stored until it needs to be traded for foodstuffs, shelter or safe passage to a less dangerous destination.

Silver

Unlike gold, the price of silver swings between its perceived role as a store of value and its very tangible role as an industrial metal. For this reason, price fluctuations in the silver market are more volatile than those in the gold market.

While silver will trade roughly in line with gold as an item to be hoarded (investment demand), the industrial supply/demand equation for the metal exerts an equally strong influence on its price.

Unlike gold, silver is predominantly used in multiple industrial applications like photography, electrical appliances, medical products, bearings, electrical connections, batteries, superconductor applications.

Platinum

Like gold and silver, platinum is traded around the clock on the global commodities markets. It tends to fetch a higher price than gold during routine periods of market and political stability, simply because it is much rarer; much less of the metal is mined annually. Other factors that determine platinum's price include:

1. Like silver, platinum is considered an industrial metal. The greatest demand for platinum comes from the automotive catalyst industry, where it is used to reduce the harmfulness of emissions. After this, jewellery accounts for the majority of demand. Petroleum & chemical refining catalysts and the computer industry use up the rest of the uses of the metal.

2. Because of the automobile industry's heavy reliance on the metal, platinum prices are determined in large part by automobile sales and production numbers. "Clean air" legislation could require automakers to install more catalytic converters, increasing demand,

but in 2009, American and Japanese car makers were turning to recycled automobile catalysts, or using more of platinum's reliable (and usually less expensive) sister group metal, palladium.

While gold ETFs are easily available for online trading in India, silver and other precious metals are still not traded online.

Financial Investment Tools	
Bank Fixed Deposits (FDs)	Stocks
Bank Recurring Deposits (RDs)	Bonds
PPF (Public Provident Fund)	Mutual Funds
EPF (Employee Provident Fund)	FMPs (Fixed Maturity Plans) of MFs
VPF (Voluntary Provident Fund)	Commodities
Gratuity	**Life Insurance**
Superannuation	Real Estate
Gold	

Life Insurance

This is one of the traditional investment tools that has often been misinterpreted. I have seen that most people do not understand the purpose of life insurance and invest money in insurance policies, looking for good returns at the same time.

Life insurance[80], or for that matter, any kind of insurance is a mechanism to provide you financial security rather than giving you returns on the invested amount. This tool is, therefore, best leveraged only if it is used for the intent of financial security for yourself and your family, in case you are not alive.

Trading in commodities is especially attractive due to the higher risk/return ratio. Commodities trades are highly leveraged, which means that the margin requirement for trading in commodities futures is quite low in comparison to overall position holding.

Therefore, it magnifies the gains and losses of an investor. Commodities prices are seeing a lot of volatility in the recent times. The price fluctuation is due to turbulence in global markets, monsoon, demand-supply mismatch and high liquidity.

Important features of a life insurance policy

There are three important aspects of any life insurance policy:

▶ **The sum assured**

This is the maximum amount of money which is secured for you or your family in case the insurance clause is triggered. Depending on the financial needs of your family, this may vary.

▶ **The term or tenure or tenor or duration of the policy**

This is the duration of the policy for which the policy is effective, unless it is short closed for non-payment of premiums or any other clause.

▶ **The premium amount**

The amount of money that you pay on a regular basis that ensures that your life insurance policy continues to be in effect and continues to provide financial security to your family.

Most people I know focus on the sum assured and compare various policies based on that, and finally select a policy based on the premium amount. The aspect that often gets ignored is the term of the policy.

Why you need life insurance?

Why do you buy life insurance? A one line answer is that your loved ones can keep enjoying the quality of life they are used to even after you are not around. Whether it is the sum assured or the tenure of the policy, this rationale is something you should always keep in mind.

What should be the term of your policy?

How do you put the above principle into practice?

You should think about the people who are financially dependent on you currently, and decide for how many years more they will remain dependent on you. You should also consider any other financial dependents that it may be necessary for you to have to support later, such as elderly parents, and decide for how many years they will need support.

For example, if you are 32 years old, have an earning spouse and a son who is 5 years old, you might need insurance only for 20 years – because by the time you turn 52, your son will be 25 years old, and should be self sufficient.

If you are 25 years old and do not have a child, you might want to take that into consideration and purchase life insurance for a slightly longer duration.

As mentioned earlier, typically life insurance should be purchased with the intent of a secure future for the family and never with the intent of high returns on the invested amount. In case your goal of buying life insurance is to put some money aside for investment, there are far better ways to do so without having to pay such commissions.

According to me, there is only one kind of life insurance that makes sense for the vast majority of us and that is term life insurance policy. This typically takes the minimum insurance premium[81] to provide maximum security but does not give you any returns. My wife has been a registered insurance provider with one of the leading life insurance provider companies and we know the 'ins and outs' of the types of insurance policies. Term Insurance is the best "value for money" as far as financial security is concerned.

With a whole life or a universal policy, on the other hand, the insurance company knows that it will almost certainly have to pay the face amount or the death benefit (and you are expected to die with it.) So, they price it accordingly.

If you have multiple existing insurance policies, you may want to terminate a few and increase your term cover so that not only are you more secure financially, but are also paying fewer premiums. The money saved thus, should be invested in better instruments as discussed in this book.

Every insurance company has a term insurance plan and this is what I would advise all of you to go ahead with.

Financial Investment Tools	
Bank Fixed Deposits (FDs)	Stocks
Bank Recurring Deposits (RDs)	Bonds
PPF (Public Provident Fund)	Mutual Funds
EPF (Employee Provident Fund)	FMPs (Fixed Maturity Plans) of MFs
VPF (Voluntary Provident Fund)	Commodities
Gratuity	Life Insurance
Superannuation	Real Estate
Gold	

Real estate can be one of the best financial investments, especially from the perspective of the return on investments.

When buying property for the purpose of investing, the most important factor to consider is the location. Unlike other investments, real estate is dramatically affected by the condition of the immediate area surrounding the property and other local factors.

Several factors need to be considered when assessing the value of real estate. This includes the age and condition of the property, improvements that have been made, recent sales in the neighbourhood, changes to zoning regulations, etc. You have to look at the potential income a house can produce and how it compares to other houses in the area.

Investment in real estate[82] makes very logical sense because it is not only your invested money that goes up, but also the money invested by the bank on your behalf from which you can profit.

Let us consider the following example to illustrate the above point.

Let us say that you purchase a home for ₹ 50 lacs. You make a down payment of around 20% and obtain the remaining 80% on loan from a bank. This essentially means that you invested approximately ₹ 10 lacs and the bank has invested ₹ 40 lacs.

Now, let us assume that the property you bought appreciated by approximately 10% a year, which is at least around the current inflation rate. Now, this is a very conservative increase in the price in a year from all accounts. If you have timed your purchase perfectly, the appreciation may be much higher. Considering even the conservative increase, in rupee terms, the appreciation in one year was ₹ 5 lacs.

Let us also assume that you pay an EMI with annual rate of

interest of around 10% to the bank. If you bought property that could be rented out, you can easily cover at least 50-75% of your EMI from Day 1. That leaves us with the bank EMI interest rate of approx 2-3%, which has not been covered by the rent. In rupee terms, this comes to around Rs.1 lac in Year 1.

So the picture after Year 1 is as follows: You invested ₹ 10 lacs and if you decide to sell after Year 1, you can sell the property at ₹ 55 lacs. If you return the principal amount of ₹ 40 lacs and Year 1 EMI interest of ₹ 1 lac, to the bank, you are left with ₹ 14 lacs. Now, that is a return of 40% on the amount the bank invested on your behalf and the appreciation that you received was not only on your amount but also on the investment of the bank's part.

This amount can be much larger if you time the investment and the location. Remember that the rent and the appreciation in the price of the property are larger in locations where there are more job opportunities.

When I invested in real estate around 8 years back, I never had this strategy in mind. It was just by sheer chance that I timed a good investment, which has grown more than 5 times in the last 8 years. I have not even considered the returns it is going to give me once I decide to sell the same.

This kind of mortgage or loan or debt that creates an asset for you is also termed as "good debt" by many financial planners. This debt is good because this debt acts like an asset since it pays you more than it takes from you.

As we come to an end of this section and before we go on to the next major section, I would suggest that you revisit the list of tools that have been covered.

The whole purpose was to introduce you to these tools and also to tell you my personal experience with investment in each of these tools. Not only that, we saw certain advantages, disadvantages and important tips to keep in mind while investing in any of these tools.

As important it is to understand the tools and technical considerations of when to invest etc., it is equally important, if not more, to educate ourselves on the softer side of wealth accumulation.

These are certain personality traits, attitudes, behaviour and guidelines that help you as much as the technical knowledge about these investment tools, if not more.

The upcoming chapter on "Principles of Wealth Accumulation" deals in detail with this softer aspect. I have mentioned these principles based on my experience and my journey towards financial freedom. I had to bring about many changes in myself, my attitude and my outlook during this journey. Some of these principles are time tested and can be followed blindly while some of them should be followed at your discretion, though they work for wealth accumulation most of the time.

4

Principles of
Wealth Accumulation

*Riches begin with a state of mind and with
definiteness of purpose.*
— ***Napolean Hill***

Before we start talking about the principles of wealth accumulation, let us go over a few facts:

1. America has millions of millionaires, out of which over 80% are first generation millionaires[83].

2. 80% of the millionaires who became millionaires through a lottery lost all their money in the next 5 years.

3. The fate of those receiving other windfalls, such as insurance claims, legal settlements, and inheritance is not much better.

4. Most of today's millionaires did not graduate with high honours. They just had fundamental graduate degrees.

5. Most of these millionaires did not even qualify for a top rated college. Warren Buffet, the self made multi-billionaire investor, was rejected by Harvard Business School.

6. Most of the highly qualified, well educated professionals act almost foolishly when it comes to personal finance.

So, if it is not luck or superior intelligence that makes a millionaire, then what does?

What is the common denominator that the wealthy have and the rest of humanity does not. It is simply this:

The wealthy understand the principles of wealth accumulation and live by them.

Some, like me, learn these principles through trial and error; some learn it from mentors, parents and coaches, whereas for some, it just comes naturally.

But whatever the source of knowledge, I neither know nor have I heard or read about a single self made millionaire who does not understand and apply the principles as explained in this section of the book.

This is good news for everyone. This means that everyone can choose to live the life he or she desires. So, the control of life and the control of your finances comes right back to you.

I am not giving you any magical formula that I created or invented. I am just outlining the fundamental financial principles that if applied, can result in serious wealth accumulation over time. These wealth principles are just like any natural laws. If we know how natural laws work, we can use them to our advantage. Similarly, once we know how this fundamental law of wealth creation works, we can use it to our advantage and accumulate all the wealth that we want.

It is all in our control and it is our choice.

If you have a strong reason to be wealthy, I can assure you that you will be unstoppable after understanding this section.

Have a strong reason

The simplest questions in life are the most difficult to answer. You must have already heard many of these questions, such as:

What do you want to do five years from now?

What are your goals in life?

Why do you need money? Why do you want to be wealthy?

What is the significance of financial freedom?

What can I do if I am actually financially free?

As common and simple as these questions sound, it is difficult to obtain the right answers for them. But at the same time, it is important to answer them, otherwise it may be difficult to survive in difficult times.

As Steve Jobs, who was the CEO of Apple, said: "It is important to have passion and love for what you are doing. You must know what is driving you to your goal. There is a simple but logical reason to know this, and the reason is that whatever you are trying to achieve is not simple. It is not easy at all. There will be times when the going will get tough. There will be times when you would feel like quitting. At that time, no technique or knowledge would work. The only element that can take you through that tough time is your love and passion for the work that you are doing, your reason or the drive behind your goal. If the reason is not strong enough, you will give up in those tough times."

So, if you are reading this book to achieve financial freedom, I am sure you must be having a strong reason as to why you want to achieve financial freedom and what you can do for your family, society, country or the world if you have this financial freedom in your hands.

I had some very strong reasons, which I will not hesitate to share with you. This goal originated because I wanted to quit the rat race I was stuck in, i.e., quit my job. The more time I spent in my job, I progressed in the so called "rat race" but at the same time, I was spending less time with my family and was taking on too much stress to sustain for extended periods. I knew I was not made for politics in a job environment. I wanted to be simple, straight and honest which was not yielding great results in my job. I was just adding stress every day to my life. The thought that one day I would need to quit my job was always in the back of my mind. To do that, I needed sufficient bank balance or financial security, and this is where the dream of financial freedom originated.

As I went about trying to fulfil this dream and achieving it step by step, I realized that I truly loved certain things in life like teaching, plants and gardening.

These later translated into my dreams and are now two of the biggest goals that I want to achieve post financial freedom.

1. Plant a million trees and contribute towards mother nature.

2. Teach underprivileged children and uplift our society.

These goals are in sync with what I love to do. Well, you may have your own vision you may want to contribute to people around you or you may want to just have that freedom to decide things on your own or just want enough money to see that your family is secure.

I keep reading more and more articles nowadays on how people are contributing to the society, country or world as a whole once they become financially free.

Following is an article, which appeared in a national newspaper on Azim Premji, the founder of Wipro.

"After having taken the company to the top and earning enough money, he has taken many initiatives to improve the education system in India. He has been able to do this because of the financial freedom that he enjoys.

After chipping in for the country's educational system for a decade, the Azim Premji Foundation (APF), run by the third richest Indian on his own money, is all set for a generous initiative. The foundation plans to start 1,300 schools across the country - two per district which will be free, impart education in the local language and be affiliated to the state board.

If the idea succeeds, it could shame India's dysfunctional public education system and perhaps inspire other wealthy tycoons to look beyond their personal status-building."

There are many articles that are published daily and there are a greater number of people today trying to do "seemingly impossible" things after they have attained their goal of financial freedom. While Bill Gates, Bill Clinton and other big names have their own NGOs and their own way of helping millions across the world, there are many smaller people who are helping others in their own way.

You have got to find your own reason for financial freedom, but once the reason is clear in your mind, you will look at life in a completely different way. You will see a life that is not only worthwhile but which will give you the "happiness" that you always wanted.

John Lennon, an English musician and singer — songwriter who rose to worldwide fame as one of the founding members of The Beatles, one of the most commercially successful and critically acclaimed acts in the history of popular music and who, along with fellow Beatle, Paul McCartney, formed one of the most successful song writing partnerships of the 20th century, shares the following views on happiness:

"When I was 5 years old, my mother always told me that happiness was the key to life. When I went to school, they asked what I wanted to be when I grew up. I wrote down "Happy". They told me that I didn't understand the assignment. I told them that they didn't understand life."

Find a strong reason for financial freedom and life will be a lot happier and worthwhile.

Decide to become wealthy

Money is power. And power in good hands is a very good thing.

Each person's definition of wealth is personal. To me, you become truly wealthy and financially independent once you have to no longer think of money.

The decision to be financially independent is ultimately yours. Most people never become wealthy and financially independent because they never decide to do so. They may hope or wish for wealth and financial freedom, but never really choose. Choice is the beginning of all journeys. As Napoleon Hill wrote in his classic book: *Think and Grow Rich:* Riches begin with a state of mind and with definiteness of purpose.

Once we decide to obtain something, the mind unconsciously begins to create the reality necessary to make the desire real. This has also been amply justified in the famous book, *The Alchemist,* which says: "When you want something with all your heart, the entire nature and surroundings will conspire to make it happen for you."

The journey of a thousand miles begins with a single step. Take your first step. Decide to be wealthy. Declare your intention by saying it loudly to yourself and your family. Write it on a piece of card and keep viewing it time and again. Declare it to your near and dear ones and your friends. Make a commitment. Love it.

Even if it feels a little awkward, go ahead and write it down. This is the first step in your remarkable journey towards financial freedom.

Start early

One of the greatest misconceptions about investing is that it takes a lot of money to make a lot of money. This is absolutely incorrect. What it takes is some money and a lot of time. Hence, time becomes the most crucial component of investing, and is also the one we tend to easily squander.

Since time is so critical, the biggest success factor in your early financial independence is to start early.

Some of you may be wondering whether you are starting too late whereas others may feel that it is too early to start thinking of savings. However, if it is a question of your financial independence, it is always worth the effort.

I started earning money at the age of 21 after completing my engineering course, but it is rare that you get this kind of wisdom or financial advice at that stage of life. Our only goal at that stage of our life seems to be settling down in our career, which is of course necessary, but if we get some guidance and advice on financial planning, it will definitely help us in the long run.

Since time is an important factor, it is critical to start early on this journey. So, gone are the days when you should start investing only after you start earning. I always advise teenagers to start investing wisely on their pocket money so that investing and financial independence become a habit.

My two daughters are 8 and 10 years today and are studying in the 3rd and 4th standards. They have their own bank accounts and they take their own decisions as to how much of their monthly pocket money they want to spend on themselves and how much they want to save or invest. They understand the principles of compounding well and have realized that the longer you keep the money and bigger the amount of money, the faster it grows. I know this will not be taught in their schools ever. So, it is all the more important that it is taught in every home. They need to learn these basic facts about money and financials as early in life as possible, because they are some of the most vital principles you will need in your day to day life but will never learn in any school or college.

"When we strive to become better than we are, everything around us becomes better too."

Imagine the example you would set to your children and family around you as you go through this journey of financial freedom. Your entire family need never face financial stress during their lifetime because of the lessons they learnt from you.

Most of our financial responsibilities arise between the ages of 32 to 50, such as marriage, children, responsibility of dependent parents, etc., and the earlier we start investing, the more it helps all of us to plan for the future challenges in that age group.

Do not ever feel that it is too late to invest. Start from the day you are "awakened". My awakening came almost 12 years after I started earning money. You have to decide yours.

Pay yourself first before you pay others

A millionaire asked one of his students who was trying to understand the concepts of wealth accumulation: "If you select a basket and put ten eggs into it each morning and take out nine eggs from it each evening, what will eventually happen?"

"It will overflow in time" replied the student.

"Why?" asked the millionaire.

The student responded, "Because each day I put in one more egg than I take out."

"Do exactly as I have suggested to the egg merchant. For every ten coins you place in your purse, take out for use but nine. The purse will start to fatten at once and its increasing weight will feel good in the hand and bring satisfaction to the soul."

"Deride not what I say because of its simplicity. Truth is always simple. This was my beginning of how I built my fortune".

The above is a simplified extract from the book – *The Richest Man in Babylon* it teaches us one of the simplest ways to make sure that we get started in the right way on our journey to financial freedom.

Some of you may immediately think of reasons for not being able to save at least 10% of your salary, but believe me, 90% of your income will be as sufficient for you as was a 100%. If you are starting early in life with this book, 10% savings can be good enough to start with but if you are starting late, then of course you need to make up for the late start and accordingly plan your savings.

There is a detailed section later in the book which can help you precisely plan the amount of money that you should save each month to achieve your goals.

While we may think that 100% of our income is ours, the fact remains that most of it goes in paying others, e.g., the electricity department, water department, phone companies, house rent, etc. This whole concept is based on the simple principle that before I pay anything to anyone, I need to pay myself and only then distribute the balance wisely among others.

So, if you get your salary cheque on the 1st of every month, please make sure that you first withdraw at least 10% of that money (if not more) and put it in your investment nest egg before you start paying any of your bills or start spending on anything else.

The calculations as to how much money would you need on a monthly basis at your age and based on your goals of the nest egg etc., are all explained later in this book. The current section focuses on adapting these principles in general so that they become a part of your daily life.

Revisit these principles as many times as you want… even after you go through the complete book and have started working on your plan. It might take some time imbibing these principles but each one of these is worth its weight in gold.

Unleash the power of compounding

If Christopher Columbus had invested $1 in 1492 at 5% "simple" interest, today it would be worth approximately $25 (a 25 times increase). If the interest on the invested $1 had been compounded annually, guess what it would be today…

Well…more than $50 billion!

Does that give you an idea of the immense power of compounding interest? To further demonstrate the immense power of compounding let me give you a more apt real life example, which you can do alongside as you read. Pull out an A4 sheet of paper. Fold it in half. That is the first fold. Now, fold it in half once again for the second fold. Imagine that you could fold it into half for another 48 times (that is a total of 50 times). I know it is not practical to make so many folds on an A4 sheet, but let us imagine that you were able to do so. Next guess and write down the approximate thickness of this sheet after 50 folds.

Well, make a guess – a few centimetres, a few metres, 100 metres, 1 kilometre?

The correct answer is that the stack of paper would be so thick that it will reach from here to the sun! That is approximately 150 million kms. And no prizes for guessing the fact that though it took 50 folds to reach the sun, it just takes one additional fold to double the thickness and come back from the sun to earth. It is hard to believe, but this is exactly why most people who may understand the definition of compound interest never "really" understand and appreciate its true power.

By definition, compounding means earning interest on interest. It is the easiest way to accumulate a lot of money. I say this is the easiest because you do not have to work for this explosion of money. It grows all by itself. The discipline that you need to do this is not hard: All you have to do is leave the money untouched. One should neither touch the principal nor the interest. This will allow the money to grow in a compounded manner, at its fastest pace.

I started with this concept very early in the earning phase of my life but unfortunately was not financially literate enough at that stage to understand the importance and significance of compounding. So, as it happens with most of us, I could not adopt the discipline of "leaving the money alone," and started using the accumulated amount in bits and pieces for the so called "necessary" activities at home, like renovation of the house, my marriage etc.

After 15 years of earning, saving and spending money, I was back to square 1. I hardly had any wealth accumulation. It was only in 2007 (I was 34 by then) when I seriously started working on my financial freedom. It was during this period, I read many books on financial freedom, wealth accumulation and retirement including some bestselling authors, which caused me to re-plan my goals, and start tracking them and use the "real" power of compounding.

Compounding unleashes its power with time and therefore the younger you start gives you an "unfair" advantage over people like me who took 15 years to understand this fundamental principle of money. Therefore, I put "start early" as the first golden rule; even before the rule of compounding power. Both these rules work hand in hand to give you an explosion of wealth which you cannot even imagine in the first few years of your savings.

Figure 16 shows an example of how "starting early" and "the power of compounding" work hand in hand to give you unprecedented incomes.

Assume you are targeting a corpus wealth of ₹ 500,000 by the age 65 and all your investments earn an average interest of 10% compounded annually. Let us see how much you have to save annually to reach this target.

Starting Age	Annual Savings needed (Rupees)
30	1,844
35	3,040
40	5,084
45	8,730
50	15,737
55	31,372
60	81,899

Fig 16: *Starting early and the power of compounding*

So, if you start 10 years late, you need to invest almost 3 times more per year and if you start 30 years late, do you think you need to invest 9 times more? No..... it is a huge 44 times more per annum to reach to your target.

When it comes to the effects of compounding, you can never make up for the lost time.

Let us look at the example shown in Fig 17. Interest starts overtaking the principal after some time and becomes multiple fold faster than it became 2 fold.

"Time" is the most crucial factor in the entire equation. Compounding is extraordinary and time and discipline are the main ingredients needed for this extraordinary impact.

The table on the facing page shows an investment of ₹ 6,000 earning a cumulative interest of 8% per year.

Year	Accumulated principle	Remarks on interest
1	6000	
2	6480	
3	6998	
4	7558	
5	8162	
6	8815	
7	9520	
8	10281	
9	11103	
10	11991	
11	12950	Accumulated interest equals your principal in 1 year
12	13986	
13	15105	
14	16313	
15	17618	
16	19027	You add another principal in 5 years

Year	Accumulated principle	Remarks on interest
17	20550	
18	22194	
19	23970	You add another principal in 3 years
20	25887	

Fig 17: *"Time" factor in compounding*

Now, these number games are not meant to scare you or to make you feel guilty about not starting sooner. They are only meant to motivate you to start saving now "through a systematic financial plan" (and not just through your savings bank account).

If you are already a regular saver with a "systematic financial plan", well then congratulations! You already have that "unfair" advantage over the others, including myself!

Respect yourself and your money

Respect attracts money, this is one of the reasons why the rich get richer. If you are respectful of your money, and do what needs to be done with it, you will become a magnet, attracting more and more money.

I am sure you have encountered people with a golden touch for money. However, this is not something you are born with. It is something you learn; you must learn to be blessed with financial freedom.

You may say, I already respect money, what else do I need to do? Well, you may feel that you do so. Take out your wallet and see how the notes are organized in it. Are they all facing different ways? Are the tens mixed with the twenties and fifties? Are they just stuffed in there, so that you have to unravel them to find out what they actually are? How you actually keep your money is where the respect for your money starts. You are expected to care for it the way you care for other important things in your life.

Get rid of credit cards

A credit card allows you to buy things which you do not want with the money that you do not have.

Most of the western world is under serious credit card debt. And India is not too far behind. We seem to be headed in the same direction. It has now become a status symbol to have a number of credit cards in your wallet.

Every household in the USA has an average credit card debt of US$ 8,024, (approximately ₹ 45,000). Do you have any credit card debt that you cannot afford to clear today itself? If yes, you need to seriously re-look at your credit cards and take a decision on them.

If you want to bring your financial life out of the unknown to the known, the first step has to be clearing all credit card debts and then getting rid of the credit card itself.

You may argue in favour of the convenience that plastic money provides. Well, you have debit cards for the same. Debit cards are different from credit cards in the sense that they allow you to spend only that money which you actually have today. All merchants, sites accept any standard debit cum ATM cards today. There is no logical reason to carry credit cards in your pocket. If you do so, sooner or later, you are liable to fall under the debt of credit cards.

As they say, everyone learns the hard way. It took me 10 years of financial stress; continuously looking at my future salary to pay the previous month's credit card debt, anxiety and a huge amount of monthly interest payments before I got the ultimate advice from none other than my spouse…who always has a very simple way of looking at things.

She asked me to get all my credit cards cancelled, some 8 years back. Since that day I have not carried a single credit card and, believe me I am much more relaxed and well off, not to mention that I am very much internet savvy and use my debit card for all online transactions and bill payments.

Life is much better and simpler with no credit card bills to pay at the beginning of each month.

In fact, getting rid of credit cards contributes immensely to your investment portfolio by stopping any leakage that may have been occurring from your nest egg even without your noticing it. Typically when you pay your credit card outstanding bills, the credit card company mentions the minimum amount that has to be paid. This minimum amount is calculated using a hefty interest rate, which is mostly never explicitly mentioned in the card statement. This interest that you keep paying to the credit card company is termed as "leakage".

Invest for cash flow instead of capital gains

We first need to understand these two terms very clearly. Let me first reiterate the definition of capital gains as defined in the earlier section of this book.

A capital gain is an income derived from the sale of any investment or "capital asset". A capital investment can be a home, a farm, a ranch, a family business, or a work of art, for instance. Agricultural land is not considered as a capital asset, unless it is situated within the limits of, or within 8 kilometres of a municipality. Investments such as shares and bonds are also considered as capital assets.

It seems quite logical to earn money through capital gains. The only thing we need to know is when the stocks or the property prices might go up so that we can sell them at a considerable profit. This form of investment may not always be the best and the most reliable way to earn money. Considering an unpredictable and volatile market, many investment gurus like Robert Kiyosaki advise investors to invest in cash flows rather than capital gains.

Extending the example of buying and selling a house to realize capital gains, a cash flow investment is aimed at buying property to rent out so that it gives you an inward cash flow of money.

Technically, Investopedia defines a cash flow as follows: "A revenue or expense stream that changes a cash account over a given period. Cash inflows usually arise from one of three activities — financing, operations or investing — although this can also occur as a result of donations or gifts in the case of personal finance. Cash outflows result from expenses or investments. This holds true for both business and personal finance.

If you can control the cash flow so that it is significantly positive over a given period of time (say a month), irrespective of any market situation (i.e., whether you have a job or not), you are on the right path to financial independence. It may sometimes be hard to invest in cash flows when everyone is investing in capital gains but in the long run, and especially during turmoil, this is always going to win.

A popular board game for children (and even adults) is "Monopoly". The idea in this game is not to buy a house or property once and then sell it later at some extra margin. To be a winner in this game, you continue to buy and keep collecting rent from your house or hotel till others land on the square in which you have a house, pay rent and go broke, and you win.

Investing in capital assets is much like the game of Monopoly. The ultimate winner is the one who invests in cash flow rather than capital gains.

Invest regularly

Just as regular exercise and good eating habits make you physically healthy, regular investments make you financially healthy. In the later sections of the book, you will find sufficient tools and spreadsheets to calculate and plan how much money you need to invest each month and for how many years to reach your financial goal.

Investments have to be a regular habit. You must continue to look at the health of your investments and change the portfolio allocation based on the changing market and environmental factors.

It is important to view investing as a process and not a one-time event. Often, one of the reasons we do not start investing sooner is because, after paying bills and spending money elsewhere, we do not think there is any money left over.

By making a habit of investing regularly you gain two major advantages.

You help manage investment risk: When you invest regularly, you protect yourself against buying too much when prices are high and help reduce the temptation to sell at a bad time – i.e., when prices are low.

You "pay yourself first". A program of regular investment ensures that you attend to your long-term plan before you are tempted to spend your money on short-term needs.

Successful investing does not mean holding your money waiting for the right time to invest or frantically trying to withdraw your money when times are difficult. By investing a set amount regularly (say once a month), regardless of the market environment, and speculations regarding investing you can harness the power of two simple, yet highly effective investing principles – dollar cost averaging and compounding.

Invest before it is taxed

We know that there are certain retirement benefits based investment tools that allow you to invest in the nest egg prior to tax deduction from your salary e.g., Employee's Provident Fund (EPF), Voluntary Provident Fund (VPS), superannuation and gratuity investments.

There is a very simple reason for investing your money before taxes are deducted, as the money that you would have paid in taxes can also earn interest for you and if you are able to utilize the power of time, soon the interest can overtake your principal amount.

So, never lose the opportunity of saving in such retirement schemes or any other Exempt, Exempt, Exempt (EEE) schemes, where all three i.e., principal, interest and withdrawals are all exempt from taxes.

Never invest on tips

My experiences on investing on tips given to me by friends during various dinner invites was a total failure. As expected I had my share of money eroded over a short period of time in the stock market, before I was able to retrieve some of it using tools like dollar cost averaging.

Never ever invest in stocks based on tips from your "well meaning" friends. Everyone has an opinion, but chances are they do not have all the facts. Somebody at work may tell you about a stock that is "really going to make you a lot of money". You know nothing about the stock but rush out and buy a hundred shares nevertheless. This is the craziest thing you could ever do.

Beware before you place your trust in a friend or relative and invest your hard earned money based on rumours and street talk.

You have your own decision making power and your own ability to judge what is going on around you. You also have the freedom to choose a right investment advisor.

My advice to beginners has always been to take paid advice available on the net, do a lot of research and then take your decision based on your market study and gut feel.

Even if you make a mistake, learn from it and become better with time. Within a few years, you will realize how to make money in stocks. There is no short cut to success. You have to go through the pain of acquiring knowledge and wisdom before you can benefit from it.

Stop procrastinating, get started

Wikipedia defines procrastination as "the act of replacing high-priority actions with tasks of low-priority, and thus putting off important tasks to a later time". Procrastination may result in stress, a sense of guilt and crisis, severe loss of personal productivity, as well as social disapproval for not meeting responsibilities or commitments. These combined feelings may promote further procrastination.

"Procrastination never won a race, received a promotion or changed the outcome of any situation."

We have all experienced it, whether it is calling the repair man to make required alterations in the house, studying at the last moment or planning your financial freedom. We always think there is another day.

Well think about this.... if a fireman procrastinated about going into a burning building to save a child it could mean the difference between life and death; if an employee decided to wait a few days to apply for a promotion, he or she might never be considered..... I could go on and on.

Procrastination turns out to be one of the worst enemies to anyone's wealth building abilities. We have an uncanny ability to procrastinate, and then justify by giving valid reasons for our decision.

It took me 3 years to make my first investment in the stock market after having mentally conceptualized the fact that I must get into it. The amount of money I now earn in one year makes me realize how much money I actually lost by starting 3 years late.

The habit of always putting off something until you can afford it, or until the time is right, or until you know how to do it is one of the greatest thiefs of joy. Once you have made up your mind - jump in.

There is a famous saying which highlights the typical situation of a person who procrastinates.

"If and When were planted, and Nothing grew."

Keep your partner informed

Nothing can be more emotionally traumatic than the loss of a dear one. It can have some financial repercussions if the deceased person had handled most of the household investments. But it can be a financially crippling nightmare if he or she never told anyone else about all these investments or never left records of what has been invested and where.

People are disorganized about their finances because they never think something will happen to them.

Lack of information and lack of interest in financial matters have been the two biggest reasons behind poor investment decisions. Now lack of communication is emerging as another key cause. Most people do not communicate their financial decisions to family members because of oversight or procrastination.

Strangely, individualism too is creeping into personal finances these days and couples are steadfastly refusing to share financial information with each other.

It pays if your family, in the event of any such tragedy, is aware of all your investments and records. All your hard work should not go to complete waste just because you did not find the time to share the financial details with loved ones.

I personally gave a detailed briefing of all my financial investments and my future plans to my spouse only when I was just 2 years away from my financial independence. Every hour spent was worth it. I feel much more safe and relaxed now. Go ahead, do it right now... Do not procrastinate; you never know what is in store tomorrow.

Be patient

A lot has already been said about the power of compound interest, but the importance of compounding can never be overstated. However, because of the way compounding works, it is very easy to lose patience. You may be saving regularly and leaving the money alone to let it grow. You feel you are doing more than your best to make sure you adhere to your plan, but the goal still seems to be far away. There will definitely be times when you may actually want to go all out and put your money in a stock in the hope that it doubles because you feel you cannot increase the money as fast as you need to.

At such times, your knowledge and understanding of the way compounding works as well as your patience will pay off. If you have understood compounding, you would have understood that you earn roughly 75% of your money in the last 25% of the tenure you have planned for financial independence.

Do not get impatient. It will just exponentially increase after some stage. Give it time. I will show you some actual charts of my own financial independence journey in later sections to help you realize how this actually works in practice. This will not only help you to understand the gains that compounding brings in but also convince you to be patient and continue to be disciplined in your investments.

Remember that becoming financially independent is not like running a sprint but is more like running a marathon. You have to be patient even if you look around and see people earning more and spending more than you. You have to be rational even if you feel enough is enough and you want to quit your job now; even if you feel that you are not even reaching close to your goals.

I am sure you must have watched a long distance race. Do you know how long distance runners start practicing? They start by running just a block or two every day. They do not even start by running or even jogging, they just walk fast. It is so very different from a 100 m or a 200 m sprint.

What smart long distance runners do not do is to go out and start running 20 kms on Day 1. They gradually build up to it.

Learning to save is a lot like this marathon race. Start slowly and keep it simple. Do not get overawed by huge goals and the millions you need for financial independence. It will come as per the plan that you have made or you will make according to the advice given in the later section of this book.

Sharpen your financial saw

Bruce Barton once said: "Sometimes when I consider what tremendous consequences come from little things.... I am tempted to think that there are actually no little things."

Here's an example from the famous book *Seven Habits of Highly Effective People* by Stephen R. Covey.

Suppose you were to come upon someone in the woods working feverishly to saw down a tree.

"What are you doing?" you ask.

"Can't you see?" comes the impatient reply. "I'm sawing down this tree."

"You look exhausted!" you exclaim. "How long have you been at it?"

"Over five hours," he replies, "and I'm beat! This is hard work."

"Well, why don't you take a break for a few minutes and sharpen the saw?" you inquire. "I'm sure it would go a lot faster."

"I don't have time to sharpen the saw," the man says emphatically. "I'm too busy sawing!"

Doesn't it sound familiar? We frequently do not have time in life to do all those "little things" which have tremendous consequences in our lives.

It's all about preserving and enhancing the greatest asset you have — you. It is about renewing the four dimensions of your nature — physical, spiritual, mental, and social/emotional. Unless we renew, rejuvenate, refresh and re-launch these dimensions with fresh enthusiasm, we may get bogged down by the operational boredom of the act we are in.

While Stephen Covey talks about this from all dimensions of nature, my reference in this book is specific to sharpening your financial saw. Learning, implementing your financial knowledge to achieve results, learning again from the results of your implementation and applying that learning back to yield better results next time is what we call a "continuous improvement" cycle in software engineering. Applying this cycle to your financial planning is a significant step by itself.

An even greater step is to continuously learn and challenge the existing paradigms, take risks and do something which keeps pace with the times. While financial principles, like any other universal principles remain the same, we need to keep ourselves updated and posted with the latest developments across the world on these fronts. These latest developments provide the context or the area where your financial thinking must work to take financially sound decisions.

Most of our mental development and study discipline comes through formal education. But as soon as we leave the external discipline of school, many of us let our minds just wander around. We do not do any more serious reading, we do not explore new subjects in any real depth outside our field of work, we do not think analytically, we do not write — at least not critically or in a way that tests our ability to express ourselves in clear and concise language. Instead, we spend our time watching television. I am grateful to television and other sources of information for the many high-quality educational and entertainment programs. They can enrich our lives and contribute meaningfully to our purposes and goals.

Like our physical body, television is a good servant but a poor master. This essentially means that if we take control of our body and do the right things with it, it can yield immense results. It is the same with television. If we take control and watch the right things on television, it can be truly beneficial. So, if you have control, these things are good servants. But if you allow them to become your masters and let them decide things on your behalf, then they are real trouble.

There is no better way to inform and expand your mind on a regular basis than to get into the habit of reading good literature. I would encourage you to go through the book, *Seven Habits of Highly Effective People* by Stephen R Covey. I highly recommend starting with a goal of a book a month, then a book every two weeks, then a book a week.

There is a very well known proverb that states: "The person who doesn't read is no better off than the person who cannot read."

Quality financial literature, like financial newspapers – online or physical, subscriptions to financial magazines, regular monitoring of the stock situation, a regular check on your portfolio balance, learning new financial terms are some of the things that can expand our paradigms and sharpen our financial saw as we read and seek first to understand. Today, the options are unlimited. You can also subscribe to online journals which give you good financial knowledge[4] and advice directly in your mail box.

If we deduce before we really understand what an author has to say, we limit the benefits of the reading experience.

Go ahead, subscribe to a magazine, read a book on financial knowledge and start the journey of enriching your mind as you apply these concepts in your day to day life.

Don't put all your eggs in the same basket

We touched upon this topic in the previous section of the book when we talked about portfolio and asset classes and how your portfolio should have diversified investment in multiple asset classes.

It is especially important to diversify your equity investments. All your debt investments should not be with a single bank or a single fund or bond. Debt investments should be diversified to reduce risk. This essentially means that you should not have all your fixed deposits with one bank.

Investing in mutual funds is a good way to spread your risk as the fund managers typically invest in a variety of stocks across multiple industries. Similarly, on the debt side, investing in FMPs is one of the best ways to hold a diversified portfolio. In case you want to diversify yourself, make sure that you do not overcomplicate things. To hold more than 2 or 3 bank accounts and maintain them can be an uphill task. Of course, once you have become financially free, you can afford to keep a financial planner who can manage this on your behalf, but till that time, my suggestion would be to follow the guidelines given below in general.

Bank accounts (Savings)	: 2 to 3 banks
Bank deposits (FDs, RDs)	: 2 to 3 banks
Mutual funds	: 3 to 4 fund companies
FMPs	: 2 to 3 fund companies
Stocks	: 20 to 30 stocks
EPF/PPF/VPF/Gratuity/SA	: 1
Gold/Commodities	: 1 to 2 securities
Life insurance	: 1 to 2 insurance providers

The above guidelines are in no way cast in stone. You can always change the numbers temporarily but my experience is that if you move too far from these guidelines, the complexity and time involved in managing these diversified service providers can easily outweigh the returns and risk mitigation achieved from this diversification.

You should wait till you become financially free and then you can leave all this to a well qualified and a professional financial planner.

Get the right attitude

Zig Ziglar, one of the renowned inspirational speakers, says: "Your attitude, not your aptitude, will determine your altitude."

Another famous quote goes like this:"Whether you think you can, or you think you cannot, you are right."

Psychological research has shown that hard work and persistence after setbacks are typically found with a constellation of other psychological characteristics, all of which prevail among wealthy and financially free respondents.

Some of these characteristics are listed below. This list is by no means exhaustive or complete. If you possess the right attitude, you will make it through in tough times:

Optimism: Most wealthy persons are optimistic about their own financial future even if the initial results have been disappointing.

Problem solving approach: Wealthy and successful people respond to challenges with problem solving approaches rather than emotional reactions. This results in less stress and more action.

Part of the solution: Wealthy and successful people are always a part of the solution rather than a part of the problem. As soon as a problem arises (which will happen for sure), they start thinking and acting on a solution to it, rather than debating on the problem itself. They do not waste time on thinking on why the problem has arisen, whether they should continue with their goals or not because of the problem, why they were "chosen" for this problem, what will happen if the problem persists, and so on.

Rather than spending their time on the problem, they will work on finding out what they need to do to mitigate the problem itself, and how to prevent this problem from re-appearing in the future. They always want to be a part of the solution.

Learning orientation: Success comes in part from minimizing the inefficiencies of trial and error, both through learning from others and learning from your own experiences. Learn not only through your successes but also through your failures.

Passion: Love your work, set meaningful goals, like what you do and do what you like.

Imagination: Make timely and appropriate changes in your thinking, plans, and methods. Show creativity by thinking of new and better ideas, and solutions to problems. Be innovative.

Courage: Have the perseverance to accomplish a goal, regardless of the seemingly insurmountable obstacles. Display a confident calmness when under stress.

Dedication: Spend whatever time or energy is necessary to accomplish the task at hand.

Win in the margins (Earn extra income)

Of all the habits and principles to financial success, this is the factor that most influences your speed towards financial independence. You may find this surprising but the age old saying is very true — "Money saved is money earned".

We may be thinking hard about how to earn more money and get the next promotion, but we may be casual about spending our money, forgetting that every penny that is saved is as important as every penny earned.

While I will discuss the various money saving strategies later in this section, I want to focus more on how we can try and diversify our current income. As quoted in an issue of "Fortune" magazine, "The millionaire mentality watches cost and tries to reduce them – and also strives to increase the production and sales and thus the overall profits."

You have to treat your financial management and your financial freedom goals as seriously and diligently as any other business and work to increase your savings by watching and controlling costs (and hence expenditure) while simultaneously working on increasing the productivity (and hence income).

To make the idea of extra income clearer, I would like to tell you a true story that I once read, while sharpening my financial saw.

There was a person who had a very peculiar habit of looking for money. He would actually ride a bicycle while looking down. As odd as his behaviour was, the most surprising result of this habit was that nearly every day, he would pick up a coin or bill from the ground. I am not asking you to replicate this habit, that would be a little weird. My point in sharing the story is that you will get what you are looking for.

When you start looking for ways to increase your income and earn extra money, you will realize that there are opportunities all around you that you never thought seriously about or even noticed.

Remember that even if you are saving 10% of your income and that additional extra income earns just 5% of your total income, you do not speed up your financial freedom by that additional 5%, but by 50%.

This is because what contributes to your financial freedom is your savings and not your income. A majority of the income goes to maintain your monthly expenditure while it is the savings that matter most to us.

The same is true about ideas that keep coming to us. All too often, we discount these ideas just because they seem too obvious or simple to us. In doing so, we tend to forget that the most brilliant ideas are almost always simple in concept. None of us will ever achieve anything extraordinary except when we listen to the whispers of our heart.

There are hundreds of examples of how people started off with a very simple idea and became an instant success. It could be as simple and huge as McDonalds which started selling burgers.

There was really nothing new in the idea but implemented so well that it is the largest such chain in the world. Another, more recent example is Facebook, a virtual place where we meet our friends across the globe, to chat, share and have fun together.

Neither was selling burgers an extraordinary or a new idea nor was chatting and sharing with friends. But both these ideas grew into phenomenal successes.

I am not saying that you have to build a business to reach this level of success. Neither am I saying that all ideas will always lead to the success that McDonalds or Facebook enjoy. What I am saying is that we must follow the whispers of our hearts and take them forward and try them out rather than holding them back in our mind. There will obviously be obstacles, issues, struggles and failures as you move forward, but this is the only way you can move forward, by succeeding step by step.

You could also say that all these people who succeeded were lucky. Of course they were lucky. Anyone who says that he or she could achieve success without luck, just on the strength of his or her ideas, hard work and intelligence is either trying to fool you or fool their self. You definitely need luck on your side to make any idea a success.

However, it is also very wisely said by one of the famous millionaires of our times: "Opportunity is a goddess who does not waste her time with the unprepared".

The bottom line is that no one can ever get lucky if he or she had not been seriously looking out for ways to increase their earning abilities. You have got to give your idea a serious try and even if you fail, it is fine. Imagine if it works. What would be the future of your children, your family and all the people that you can help with the money that you can generate with a successful idea? You would also need luck but you will have to first prepare yourself and try it out. It is not that complicated. Do not be afraid of failure.

Opportunities to earn that additional income and increase your retirement amount by more than 50% are all around you. Be on the lookout. It could be in the form of doing some surveys every month that pay you, it could be taking some weekend coaching classes, or any other idea that you have, based on your strengths and abilities. Go ahead and implement that idea. It can have an unbelievable impact on the speed at which you can be financially free.

Win in the margins (Increase your savings)

Coming back to the age old saying "Money saved is money earned," a   millionaire mentality always recognizes that the world is designed to take our money. We have been psychologically conditioned to consume and spend. Marketers and salesman are studying your spending patterns and targeting you so that you are inspired to spend more and more. In fact the target is more focussed on the younger generation which does not understand the whole concept of financial planning, savings and financial freedom.

This millionaire mentality can be applied to all aspects of a financial endeavour, from business to personal spending.

Remember the amount of money that you save is absolutely equal to the amount of extra money that you would have earned. So, never think that the act of saving money is anything less than the act of earning more money.

If you have saved ₹ 100 in buying a shirt, you just earned ₹ 100 extra. That sounds more lucrative. Ultimately, it is this saved money that is going to contribute to your financial freedom savings, just as if you had earned an extra income. So, generally, if you save 10% of your income for financial freedom and somehow you could now save 12% (which is an additional 2%), you have just brought forward your retirement by 20%.

Some of the golden rules you can use to ensure that you have saved money when spending anything, are given below. Some may involve changing some of your spending habits but they are worth it.

1. **Seven golden words**

   Whenever you are about to spend any money, always look for an opportunity to see how cheaply you can purchase – especially big items. Do take the time to compare prices and ask for special discounts before finalizing a purchase.

   Just seven simple golden words like "Is that the best you can do?" are likely to provide surprising success. As consumers, we leave a lot more money on the table than we think. We may hesitate to ask for discounts but it is worth all the effort. These 7 golden words do not require any haggling. In fact the more softly and kindly you use them, the better they work, simply because it does not create a confrontational approach.

2. **Check your expenditure**

   Of course, all expenditures cannot build your assets. But continuously asking questions like; "Is this expenditure contributing to my wealth?" helps to redirect the use of your money. It is no coincidence that the wealthy put the money in their homes instead of their cars. Homes usually appreciate while cars almost never do.

3. **Is this an impulse purchase?**

   Impulse buying is the mainstay of retail establishments. There are many famous sayings, which are all true, such as:

   "Never shop with an empty stomach."
   "Never shop without a checklist of items."

Like most of us who do not understand the importance or the habits of a millionaire, I have suffered many times in my life because of this impulse buying before I was financially educated on this aspect. I had signed up for many credit cards and club memberships (like Club Mahindra) just because of aggressive selling by the salesman. It is another matter that I had to later cancel my membership and take a refund (after losing some of the money.)

My wife and I took a pledge later that whenever we encountered any sales pitch where we had to buy "right now" or lose the opportunity, it would be empowering to be able to say no. And we have done this successfully now for more than 10 years.

With this, we conclude one of the extremely important sections of this book. All these success principles, listed in this section, may not be new to you and you may have already implemented some of them in your life. You should be aware of these principles but not to get into the habit of following them and living by them.

They seem simple. But let me give you a word of caution. If you are already not using these financial success principles in your life, trust me it is also not going to be easy. You will face all kind of challenges and priorities when you start implementing them in your own life. It is not only you but your family, relatives and friends who will feel the impact. You will have to change for this to work. I have already stated this point in the beginning of this book. What keeps so many people from becoming financially free? The principles are simple and straight forward. The most difficult part is to bring about that change in yourself.

I am not trying to de-motivate you. I am only trying to prepare you for the change that you must bring about in yourself if the goals and dreams for which you are working are important to you.

The question you need to ask yourself is whether the discomfort of changing yourself and sacrificing the smaller things in life for a bigger objective is worth the effort or not. If it is, if your dreams are important, if your goals are different from others, you will have to do things differently.

I still remember some instances, which made me think and ultimately made me focus more on my goals. I have no hesitation reproducing some of these incidents here. There were times when my colleagues in the office, who are aware of financial freedom and how to achieve it, would show me their new car and their new mobile phones. Some of these colleagues were working for me and I was their supervisor. Some of them even went to the extent of telling me that it was high time I bought a new car or the latest mobile phone. They even told me that my current car and phone do not suit my stature. I had to simply listen to them and smile. This was possible without causing me undue stress because the only thing that I focussed on at that time was my goal, my dream in life.

There were instances when my neighbours bought better cars than I did. It is not that I could not afford one or would not enjoy having one. Who does not like to give himself and his family all the comforts that one could afford. I was definitely earning more than my colleagues. But the question was of happiness. Being financially stable and approaching my goals in life gave me a different kind of joy and happiness. I could stand all that because I was passionate and focused about my goals.

It is therefore important to remember why you are doing all this. Why do you want to be financially free? You need to have passion and love for your final goals, as in difficult times, it is this that will lead you to the right decisions and response.

I want to share another important aspect of this beautiful journey.

If you are married and have children, make sure that you

openly discuss your goals and dreams with your spouse and children. Share how you intend to achieve these goals in your life and how this will impact them in future.

There are many strong reasons to do this, first and foremost is the fact that you cannot complete this journey without their support. During the times when you manage with an old car, your family also has to sacrifice. However, if they are not clear on the reason for this, they may not appreciate the struggle and therefore may not like it. The journey will actually become very difficult without their active support and involvement.

Secondly, your children will be your best teachers in times of distress and the times you fall behind in your goals. There were many times when my 8 and 10 year old daughters would help me to rise back from a failure by reminding me of some happy incidences which would instantly rejuvenate me. They will be your greatest strength. I have seen my children trying to save money, avoid pizzas over the weekend and do whatever they could to help me achieve what I want to achieve. All this is because they know how important it is for me, because I have openly shared my dreams and goals with them and they are involved in each of my successes and failures.

Thirdly and most importantly, it is imperative that you pass on whatever you have learnt to the next generation. If you work with them as a team, you do not actually need to really sit down and teach them. They will learn from you every day. I can only tell you that if your children learn how to dream, how to set goals and how to achieve them, you will cherish this journey.

The journey will be difficult, so you have to prepare for it. We will see how to set smaller milestones in the next section. You must celebrate these smaller milestones whenever you achieve them during the journey. This will not only add spice but your near and dear ones will eagerly await your next milestone. This will motivate you as well.

The next section is very special to me. It is my personal journey from the rat race to financial freedom.

My recommendation is not to hurry through the next section. Work on your own plan as you go through the next section step by step. If you face any difficulties in preparing your plan, please visit the website at www.ratrace2freedom.com or feel free to write to me at help@ratrace2freedom.com.

Once you are ready with your plan, please reread the book at least once. During your journey, you should refer to the book as and when you need to. Besides you must sharpen your financial saw by subscribing to a regular update at your website. Do not hesitate to refer to other financial informative mails, websites or magazines. Acquire as much knowledge as you can. Challenge yourself. Ask questions. Acquire knowledge and then take your own decisions.

5

Financial Freedom Planning and Tracking

Those who plan do better than those who do not plan even though they may not be able to stick to their plan.

— ***Winston Churchill***

We are now familiar with all the financial investment tools, the practices of millionaires and some key fundamental concepts that we need to inculcate in our daily life so as to accumulate serious wealth.

Let us now come to the most important aspect in the journey towards financial freedom, namely creating your own financial independence plan, which is practical, achievable as well as challenging. This aspect is also about starting to track your actual results against the plan and making sure you always stay on track.

Achieving your end goal requires meticulous planning along with disciplined and consistent investments. It also means revisiting your portfolio and investment strategies to ensure that your plan is not being derailed by external factors like market forces and interest rate variables. We are going to deal with real numbers and real money now.

Below are the eight steps to financial independence. These steps are arranged in a specific sequence, which you must follow. Do not jump the gun. Believe me, there is no short cut. Whenever you are confused or stuck, look out for help. Do not go to the next step till you have worked out your plan up to the step which you have read. If you do not implement the plan and just read through this section of the book, you will not gain anything.

This section of the book is intended to help and handhold you to prepare your own plan and a mechanism to track your plan.

I will walk with you on each of these steps and share with you my experiences and learning as I went about the journey of becoming a "financially free" man.

Eight Steps to Financial Independence Planning

Step 1: Establish your cash flow

Calculate your cash inflow (what you get every month) and outflow (what you spend every month).

Step 2 : Identify your assets, liabilities and net worth

Determine how much money you have today counting all possible assets and liabilities.

Step 3 : Create a high level financial freedom plan

Estimate and assess the size of your nest egg, which will be adequate to sustain your expenses and taxes, as well as take care of inflation for the rest of your life. Take the time needed to build this nest egg.

Step 4 : Create a detailed financial freedom plan

Create a month on month portfolio plan that ties up with your high level financial freedom plan in Step 3.

Step 5 : Execute the financial freedom plan

Once you have a plan in place, it is time to execute it. For each asset class in your portfolio, I will give you some important tips to execute your plan.

Step 6 : Track your financial freedom plan monthly

Track the monthly nest egg target against the actual nest egg value on a regular basis and make sure that you stay on track.

Step 7 : Tune your portfolio breakup for the coming year

Use trends based on the last year and previous years to

see which part of the portfolio is giving best returns, and make your next year's investments based on that.

Step 8 : Celebrate milestones with your family

Celebrate each small milestone during your journey with your family and friends and give yourself a pat on the back.

These are the eight simple steps to make or break your dreams.

Follow me as I take you through my journey with each of the steps. Do not hesitate to stop, re-read and understand each step before you move on to the next step. Do visit the website http://www.ratrace2freedom.com for any clarifications that you may need, but remember, in the end, it is all about you, your dream, your goals and what you want to do with your life. If you want to make your life significant, just go for it. It is possible and you have God's permission to do so!

Step 1: Establish your cash flow

We all work hard for our money, yet we do not let it work for us because we simply do not deal with it. And not dealing with the money is just another way of dealing with it i.e., badly.

I can understand that it is not easy for you to believe or digest this. You might feel you are doing a good job already by earning money and spending it wisely. But I am going to ask you some very simple, logical questions, which you should answer honestly.

How much does it cost you precisely to live each month?

How much are your net family savings each month?

If you have a partner in life, ask him or her to write the answers to the same two questions. If you find them difficult to answer or feel that the questions are not important, then I must congratulate you. You are now one step closer to what you need to do to make a plan for your financial freedom. You are now also aware as to what happens with 98% of the people and why they cannot be financially free irrespective of their earnings. It is because they are not in control of what is happening to their financial life. They "seem" to have control but actually have "none".

The first and the most important task is to understand where you stand today in the cash flow. This simply means you need to precisely understand your cash inflow and cash outflow as of today.

Unless you are an astute planner, you probably never had the time to do this "useless" calculation, or you did some calculations a few months back. The latter is useless if you have not utilized the information or data to your benefit. If these calculations are still lying on some rough paper, or somewhere in your laptop, or in a stack of papers you have not looked at for a long time, it is time to take them out and review them because your financial independence is at stake and it is worth putting in another attempt.

Another situation that may arise is that you have your calculations ready but you are still not in control of your finances. This may be due to the fact that you never linked your calculations to your dreams. May be you did not cover expenses that do not occur at regular intervals or expenses that just crop up time and again.

Whatever the reason and whatever your current state let us start from scratch. I will take you through this journey step by step. I cannot emphasize how important it is that you should not move to the next step till you are comfortable with the first step and have worked out your own numbers and calculations for the first step.

Establish cash outflow

You must think about your money. Who cares more about your money than you? It is time to face the truth and do so honestly. This is essential. This is the foundation step to your entire financial dream.

Go through all your cheque books, account statements, ATM statements, credit card bills and anything else that tells you how you spent your money over the last 2 years. It will take some time to do this, but will give you time and money in the future. It is the end result or the goal that must drive your actions today. You should look at the amount over the last 2 years so that you arrive at a more realistic cash outflow statement. You work 40 hours a week or more to earn money. I am asking you to take a few hours to bring your money out of the darkness into the light of reality. Do not just read this and do not move ahead. Pick up a pen and paper and take action.

Do you remember the example earlier in the book where a person cutting trees did not have the time to sharpen his saw? I just hope you do not continue to be so busy in the process of earning money that you do not have a few hours to realize what is happening to all the money that you are earning, what your current state of cash flow is, and where you are headed.

Start thinking, start writing. Some of the points below may help you but do not finish this exercise in a hurry. It concerns your financial freedom. You are trying to achieve something extraordinary in life, something that only 2% of people in the world ever achieve. Nothing worthwhile can be achieved without enough sacrifice. You have to take this very seriously. Therefore, a realistic number now will help you plan better.

Let us go through some of the points that will enable you to come up with the correct cash out flow. As you go through these points, just start jotting down the cash value of the answer. Some points may not be applicable to you. Strike them out after careful thought.

I will give you a working template sheet later to help you write all this down very systematically but as of now, just start scribbling these numbers based on whatever data you have with you.

Points to check regarding cash outflow

- ► How much do you spend on groceries?

- ► Are you living in a rented apartment? How much rent you are paying monthly? Are there any annual charges as well?

- ► Do you have any outgoing EMIs every month? Do you default in paying them sometimes leading to additional charges?

- ► Do your children's school fees include annual charges as well as transportation charges? What about expenses on their school uniforms and school books?

- ► Is there a regular routine expenditure to get school homework done for your children?

- ► Do your children go for summer camps and other tuition classes?

- ► Do your children often apply for other competitive exams which cost you fees for registration and books and/or tuitions?

- ► Do you maintain a garden or a lawn? How much do you spend on it?

- ► Do you belong to a gym? Include monthly expenses as well as any annual renewal charges.

- Do you wear disposable contact lenses? Cover monthly expenses as well as any annual renewal charges.

- Do you pay any insurance premiums? The premiums could be for life insurance, vehicle insurance, home insurance and medical insurance.

- Where did you go on vacation last year? Do you go regularly for vacations?

- Do you pay someone to do your taxes each year?

- What are the values of your electricity and water bills? Do they have a predictable variance over the year?

- Do you get your car serviced regularly?

- How much fuel does your car consume monthly?

- What are your regular health check up expenses for you and your family?

- How much do you spend on clothes?

- How much do you spend on books and other toys for your children on a regular basis?

- Do you have a servant/s in your house?

- Do you have an internet and telephone connection at home?

- What are the TV cable charges?

- How much is your mobile bill? Do you change your mobile every year?

- Do you go out for movies and dinners regularly?

- Do you regularly donate some money to charitable institutions?

- Do you smoke?

- Do you have a membership with a sports club which needs renewal or payment at a regular frequency?

- Do you have any magazine and newspaper subscriptions?

- How much do you spend on special occasions, like gifts and bouquets for birthday parties and marriages?

- Does your health insurance cover you 100%? If not, it is better to factor in your part of the insurance in your annual expenses.

The list can be even more elaborate. The more time you spend on this now, the closer you will be to reality and your financial independence plan will be more accurate. Brainstorm with your family, let everyone contribute; wait for a day or two and then review your answers so that you do not miss out on some of the seemingly small expenses that accumulate to big ones.

Finally, you need to allocate 5 to 10% of your planned expenses each month for miscellaneous and unpredictable expenses.

When I did this exercise for myself, I was shocked to discover how much I had underestimated my monthly expenses.

Figure 18 shows a snapshot of the exercise I did in March 2007 when calculating the cash outflow. This spreadsheet lists each expense head, whether big or small.

ID	Amount	Title	Tenure	Remarks
M01	15033	Home Loan EMI	Monthly	
M03	1250	Life Insurance	Monthly	MNYL Policy No.
S01	3000	Life Insurance	Semi-Annual	MNYL Policy No.
M04	50	Trash Picker	Monthly	
M05	700	Maid	Monthly	
M06	170	Car Wash	Monthly	
M07	500	Tution Fees	Monthly	Harshita
M08	2500	Conveyance	Monthly	Petrol, Diesel, Parking
M09	1500	Eat Out	Monthly	
M10	1300	Mobile	Monthly	Manoj
M11	1500	Mobile + Internet	Monthly	Poonam
M12	1000	Gifts	Monthly	
M13	2500	Shopping	Monthly	
M14	9000	Grocery	Monthly	
M15	1000	House Maintenance	Monthly	
M16	500	Clothes Ironing	Monthly	
M17	1000	Entertainment	Monthly	
M07	500	Tution Fees	Monthly	Arushi
M18	1000	Kids extra curr	Monthly	
M19	1500	Medical expenses	Monthly	
M20	400	LPG	Monthly	
B01	2500	Elec Bills	Bi-Monthly	
A01	4000	House Tax	Annual	
Q04	6000	Car Maintenance	Quarterly	
M24	65000	Target 1 Cr Saving	Monthly	
M26	24125	House Renovation Loan	Monthly	

Fig 18: *Cash flow outflow spreadsheet*

The results may come as a shock to some of you, but there is a wonderful flip side to this exercise. Once you take this step, you will feel better now that you know the truth, and you will slowly begin to gain power over money which had been controlling you for such a long time.

Do not worry about creating new templates in Excel. All templates illustrated in this book are available to all book owners at no additional fees on the website: http://www.ratrace2freedom.com

Alternatively, you may opt to use something of your own. It is totally up to you. You must use what works for you.

Now that you know your exact expenses every month, it is time to monitor the incomes or inflow, and hope that the income is significantly more than the expenses. It is now time to face the reality.

Establish cash inflow

The second step is to write down the incoming cash flow from every source. Please take care to calculate and write down an amount for income heads for which you are fairly certain that the income will continue to come in for at least another year. For example, do not predict the future price of stocks and assume that you will make a profit and consider that as a part of your income.

Again, be as realistic as possible to how much you can really count under each head.

Possible sources of income could be:

▶ Monthly pay cheques after tax deduction.

▶ Predictable bonuses

▶ Income from fixed deposits, bonds and dividends

▶ Rental income, in case you have any

▶ Pension income

▶ Any gifts/regular incoming cash from your parents and relatives

You can use the same spreadsheet of cash outflow (Figure 18) for cash inflow with the incomes as you noted down now.

Once your cash inflow spreadsheet is complete, you are now ready with all expenses and incomes for each month. You are now done with the first part of this exercise. I want to re-emphasize here that you should not be in a hurry to complete this exercise. Spend time in laying a strong foundation. Typically, if you have never done this detailed exercise before, it will take you at least 1 to 2 weeks to do it justice. During these 2 weeks, keep monitoring where you use your card, cash, cheque etc., and whether or not you have written down all those expenses in your cash flow sheet.

Once completed, this exercise either re-confirmed that you were in total control of your finances already or more likely (as is the case for most of us), it confirmed that we spend more than we ever thought, if not more than what we earn.

So, now, you exactly know how much money you are capable of saving per month (monthly inflow minus monthly outflow) to reach your target for financial independence. However, you are not yet done. The hard part, which needs a lot of discipline, starts now.

We have done the calculations just to make sure that we are not out of sync with reality and that these calculations make sense, let us do the exercise below before we go to Step 2 of financial planning. Let us find a mechanism to track and make sure that this exercise was not just a theoretical calculation but a realistic representation of your income and expenditure.

From the 1st of the coming month, and for at least 2 months from now (and if feasible continuing for a year), keep a track of each expense and income in your house hold. You can do this by creating a table on a simple sheet of paper or you can do it in a spreadsheet in Microsoft Excel.

Figure 19 shows a snapshot of the monthly expense tracking sheet that I use to keep track of my cash flow (inflow as well as outflow) to make sure that I am in control of my expenses and to know whether my actual savings per month match what I had calculated in the previous exercise.

Day	Category	Title	Amount
28-May-11	Income	IN_IBM Salary	
29-May-11	Expense	House Maintenance	
29-May-11	Expense	Grocery	
29-May-11	Expense	Travel and Outings	
30-May-11	Expense	Kids extra curr	
30-May-11	Expense	House Maintenance	
30-May-11	Expense	Grocery	
30-May-11	Expense	Electricity Bills	
31-May-11	Expense	Entertainment	
31-May-11	Expense	Shopping	
31-May-11	Expense	Grocery	
01-Jun-11	Expense	Internet and Vonage	
01-Jun-11	Expense	Eat Out	
02-Jun-11	Expense	Eat Out	
03-Jun-11	Expense	Rent for Apptt	
03-Jun-11	Expense	Grocery	
04-Jun-11	Expense	Grocery	
05-Jun-11	Expense	Shopping	
05-Jun-11	Expense	Grocery	

Fig 19: *Monthly expense tracking*

Regular daily tracking through the above tracker or a similar tracker, will give you the confidence that you are in real control of your money – at least of the way it comes in and goes out every day. It is a great feeling knowing exactly how much money comes in and how much money goes out.

Remember your goals and dreams. It is time to look at them again as you start taking more control of your money. You are about to take step by step actions to make these goals a reality.

A detailed spreadsheet for tracking your actual daily/monthly income or expense tracking can be downloaded from the website: http://www.ratrace2freedom.com.

Step 2: Identify your assets, liabllities and net worth

The key to any financial planning process is to know your net worth[84].

In very simple terms, net worth is the total value of everything you own (your assets) minus everything you owe (your liabilities). Once you are able to calculate your net worth and you also know your cash flow, it is possible for you to calculate and plan how much you need to save on a yearly or monthly basis to reach your target of financial freedom.

List your assets

What is an asset?

Anything that you own is an asset[85]. It could be the house you live in, it could be your car or your sofa or it could even be your good behaviour (a non materialistic asset).

Which assets are counted?

You are identified in society by the material and non material assets that you possess. However, to keep things simple and within the perspective of the topic of financial planning and financial independence, we will focus on only those assets that are available to help you become financially independent. So, if you are driving a car that you own and will continue to drive the same after you are financially independent, it is not counted as an asset for the simple reason that I cannot liquidate the asset and invest in potentially higher earnings.

So, while counting your assets, please discount all assets that you cannot liquidate[87] after you become financially independent. Typical examples could be the house you are going to live in, your fridge, sofa etc. Other houses that you own, which can be liquidated, are counted as assets.

Be conservative while assessing the value of an asset

Remember to be on the conservative side while counting the value of an asset, for the simple reason that when you want to liquidate them, you will never get the market value of the specific asset you are going to liquidate. So, be realistic and jot down the least amount you are likely to receive in case you have to liquidate the asset post your financial independence.

Figure 20 shows a list of assets that I had listed while calculating my total assets. Only those assets were counted that could be liquidated after financial freedom was reached. Note than some of the life insurance policies are listed as assets with the amounts post their maturity. The premiums for these policies will be liabilities till their maturity date.

AssetID	Title	Amount [Rs.]	Remarks
5	Indica Car		Estimated market value of the Car (assuming a depreciation @ 10% annually) {01-10-2011}
6	Dwarka House		Estimated Market value of the Flat at Kalka Appts {01-06-2012}
9	Life Insurance Policy - Arushi Arora		Arushi to rec. the foll. % of 1L on ages : 18 yrs - 20%, 20 yrs - 20%, 22 yrs - 30%, 24 yrs - 30% {01-01-2007}
10	Life Insurance Policy - Harshita		Policy maturity value when Harshita reaches the age of 18 years {01-01-2007}
11	Gold in Bank Locker		Approx cash equivalent {01-04-2011}
15	Kisan Vikas Patra - Harshita		Due Date : Feb 2013
16	Life Insurance - Harshita		MNYL Policy done by Poonams Mom / Dad for which we pay Rs. 700 semi-annually {01-01-2007}
17	Life Insurance - ULIP - Manoj Arora		Sum Assured / Death Benefit as on year 0 {01-01-2007}
19	Life Insurance - Whole Life - Manoj Arora		Sum Assured / Death Benefit as on Year-1 {01-01-2007}
21	Target 2CR - FDs*MFs* GTEFs* Stocks* PPF*EPF*SA		As on 01-07-2012
	Total [Rs.] :		

Fig 20: *Assets table*

An actual detailed spreadsheet with the template for tracking your assets can be downloaded from the website http://www.ratrace2freedom.com

List your liabilities

What is a liability?

Anything that you owe is a liability[86]. It could be the EMIs of the house, premiums of insurance policies, credit card bills and any other cash outflow that you are aware of.

Figure 21 shows the list of liabilities that I kept a track of (and still do) for calculating my total liabilities.

AssetID	Title	Amount [Rs.]	Remarks
8	Dwarka House home loan		Pending 151 EMIs @ Rs.15033/- each {01-07-2012}
10	Insurance Policy Premiums - Harshita		MNYL Policy Semi-Annual Prem : Rs.3000. Validity:June 2021. To pay = 26 @ Rs.3000/- {01-01-2009}
11	Insurance Policy Premiums - Arushi		LIC Policy Semi-Annual Prem : Rs.2695. Validity:May 2019. To pay = 22 @ Rs.2695/- {01-01-2009}
12	Harshita MNYL Policy	•	45 Equated Installments every 6 months @ Rs.700 [Balance is paid by Poonam Mom and Dad] {01-02-2007}
13	Life Insurance - ULIP - Manoj Arora		MNYL Policy Monthly Prem : Rs.1250. Validity:July 2040. To pay = 31 @ Rs.15000/- pa. {01-01-2009}
14	Life Insurance - Whole Life - Manoj Arora		MNYL Policy Quarterly Prem : Rs.2750. Validity:July 2073. To pay = 65 @ Rs.11000/- pa. {01-01-2009}
15	HDFC Life Cover		Rs. 6500 pa * 63 years{till the age of 99} Updated as on 01-02-2011
Total [Rs.] :			

Fig 21: *Liabilities table*

The actual detailed spreadsheet for tracking your liabilities can be downloaded from the website http://www.ratrace2freedom.com

Calculate your net worth

What is a net worth?

Assets minus liabilities give you your net worth.

How often you must update your net worth?

Net worth changes with time, as you save more, invest more or spend more with time. It thus becomes important to monitor your net worth at regular defined intervals. It is extremely important that you update your net worth since it directly influences your plan for financial freedom and the time it will take to achieve the same.

I still continue to do these updates to my net worth once a month. But at the very least, it should be done once a quarter. If you are on a fast track to financial independence, I recommend updating this once a month. After you have done the hard work of creating your assets and liabilities table once, and calculated the net worth from the same, it does not take lot of time to do regular updates every month.

It is very interesting, as well as important, to keep a month on month chart of your net worth and see if you are on the right track and your net worth is continuously going up.

Step 3: Create a high level financial freedom plan

"Plan the work and work the plan" was our success mantra as project managers in the software industry. What it essentially means is that the first step is to plan the work before starting to execute the work. In our daily life, and similarly with financial planning, we are often tempted to get started fast and not "waste" our time on planning.

But it has been proven time and again that a good plan is half the battle won.

Once a clear and definite plan is ready, we need to work on that plan, stick to it and strive hard to achieve or over achieve the plan.

It will also make you think of innovative ways to meet the targets in the plan in case you are behind on any specific activity in the plan. You can use any project planning tool to create your financial plan or as I did it, you can use a simple Excel spreadsheet to plan your financial independence and then use the same to track the actual progress as compared to the plan.

When it comes to planning and that too if it is planning for your financial independence, we need to make sure that the plan is Specific, Measurable, Attainable, Realistic Timely (SMART). In the next section you will see in detail how to develop such a plan.

High level financial independence plan

Planning starts at a high level and needs certain key inputs from the previous sections to proceed.

Creating a high level plan essentially needs the following mandatory inputs:

1. Starting point (your current net worth)

2. End point (amount of money needed to become financially free)

3. Time to reach from the starting point to the end point (this will depend on the cash inflow and cash outflow each month or each year)

Let us look at each of these steps in detail.

Starting point

This is the amount of money that you start with to move towards your journey on financial independence.

We just did an exercise in the last section to determine our net worth. That is precisely what we need to know to determine our starting point. The higher your net worth the better is your start.

Do not get de-motivated in case you are starting with a low net worth or even starting from scratch. There are many more important factors that determine how fast you can achieve your goals. But yes, having a high net worth to start with is definitely a positive start.

End point

This is the amount of money that you need to end up with which can trigger your independence and will also help you sustain your nest egg for the rest of your life and continue to provide you with enough money every month covering all your expenses, inflation and taxes.

The factors that impact the decision of the size of the nest egg that you need to have at the time of your financial independence are given below.

While reading this, do not worry how you will calculate the amount of your nest egg, given these factors. We will come to that later. First, you just need to understand and put into the right perspective as to what inputs are needed to calculate the amount you require.

1. Freedom start year
   a. This is the year in which you plan to start your financial freedom.
   b. As of now, make the best guess and decide a year. If needed, we will revise it later in our spreadsheet based on the results.

2. Annual inflation rate

   a. This rate is extremely important to determine the continuing increase in your expenses every year. You can look at some government websites or search the Internet or look at cost inflation index figures to get an approximate idea of the average rate of inflation over the last few years.

   b. Your monthly expenses increase every year and are deducted accordingly from the nest egg.

3. Last year of life

   a. Well, let us face it. You have to plan how long you are going to live.

   b. This has a big impact on the nest that you need to accumulate since it must be large enough to last until the end of your life.

   c. Assume an average life span based on your country or city. To be on the safer side, assume at least 10 years on the higher side so that you have enough money in case you live longer than planned.

4. Monthly expenses

   a. These are the monthly living expenses at the start of your financial freedom year that will maintain your current standard of living throughout your freedom years.

   b. These data are used to determine the annual expenses that come from your nest every year.

   c. These expenses also keep increasing each year depending on the annual inflation rate.

   d. This amount has a drastic impact on the value of the nest egg that you must create to get a financial impact.

5. Return on investments

    a. This is the return that you can expect on your nest egg every year, based on your portfolio investment.

    b. Even in a very conservative plan, it is safe to assume returns of 9 to 10%.

    c. Every year, the returns will keep pushing the nest egg up while inflation as well as monthly expenses will keep pushing it down. In this fight between return on invested portfolio and "inflation + expenses", the nest egg must survive long enough (till you are alive).

    d. As we said earlier in the book, the whole idea of investments is to continue to beat inflation and become richer every day.

Before you go further, try and go through all the inputs needed to calculate the amount in your nest egg once again. Think as to whether you have all the inputs readily available for your case. If not, take a break here and obtain the inputs before you proceed further.

Once you have the above numbers, the calculation of a nest egg is not that complex. The procedure is given below. Even if you do not fully understand the procedure, do not worry, you can download the calculation sheet from the website http:// www.ratrace2freedom.com

If you provide the above inputs to the "Nest Egg Calculator" sheet, it will automatically calculate and provide you with the nest egg needed to start your financial freedom and the year on year nest egg balance till the last year of your life.

Procedure for nest egg calculation (in case you do not have the Nest Egg Calculator)

    a. Assume an approximate nest egg figure.

b. Reduce the nest egg figure every year by your annual expenses.

c. Increase the nest egg figure by the return on investments expected on the balance nest egg amount.

d. Arrive at the nest egg balance next year.

e. Continue to increase your annual expenses according to the rate of inflation every year and keep reducing the amount from your nest egg.

f. Keep adding the returns on investments to the nest egg.

g. Continue to do this exercise from Steps a to f for the number of years you expect to live after achieving your financial independence.

h. If in any of the years, your nest egg balance becomes negative, this clearly indicates that you did not have a sufficient nest egg to start with. You must have more money in your nest egg before you can declare yourself financially free.

i. Try the same exercise by increasing the value of the nest egg and see if it can survive for the rest of your life after reducing expenses and adding returns each year.

j. You can continue to tweak parameters like rate of inflation, expenses per month, rate of returns and then see the impact of these variations on your nest egg balance each month.

This is easier said than done. To make this entire exercise a little simpler for all of you, I have created a small worksheet which takes the above mentioned inputs and based on these inputs, it tells you the nest egg balance at the end of each year of your life. In an Excel spreadsheet, trying different values of your nest egg and other parameters becomes much easier.

Figure 22 is a snapshot of the inputs that I used for my nest egg calculation in this nest egg calculator. In the beginning, many of the values in this table can be a best guess for you but you will need to tune these guesses based on the results that you get for these inputs.

Input Description	Input Value
Nest Egg Amount	1,65,00,000
Inflation Rate	7%
Independence Start Year	2014
Last Year of Life	2063
Monthly Expense in 1st year	50000
Annual Return on Investments	10%

Fig 22: *Inputs to nest egg calculator*

Once you tune your above inputs fairly accurately, the Nest Egg Calculator will give you the nest egg balance each year.

Once you give the above inputs as in Fig 22, the Excel spreadsheet shows you a table as in Fig 23.

Points to Remember:

1. If any of the numbers in Column 2 (the amount at the end of the year) in Fig 23 give a negative value, it simply means it is time to tune your nest egg inputs in Fig 22.

2. Normally, you would not tamper too much with inflation rate, last year of life or annual returns on investments.

3. You will definitely need to adjust one or more of amounts in your nest egg, independence start year, and monthly expenses in the 1st year.

4. If the numbers in Column 2 (the amount at the end of year) in Fig 23 give a continuously increasing value till the

end of your life, then probably you have overestimated your nest egg. You will need to tune it.

5. This exercise to strike the right balance between all input parameters may take some time. Give it the required time.

End of Year	Amount at end of Year	Expenses per Year	Balance after Expenses
2014	1,74,90,000	6,00,000	1,59,00,000
2015	1,85,32,800	6,42,000	1,68,48,000
2016	1,96,30,446	6,86,940	1,78,45,860
2017	2,07,84,962	7,35,026	1,88,95,420
2018	2,19,98,333	7,86,478	1,99,98,485
2019	2,32,72,482	8,41,531	2,11,56,802
2020	2,46,09,248	9,00,438	2,23,72,044
2021	2,60,10,358	9,63,469	2,36,45,780
2022	2,74,77,390	10,30,912	2,49,79,446
2023	2,90,11,746	11,03,076	2,63,74,315
2024	3,06,14,601	11,80,291	2,78,31,456
2025	3,22,86,859	12,62,911	2,93,51,690
2026	3,40,29,098	13,51,315	3,09,35,544
2027	3,58,41,510	14,45,907	3,25,83,191
2028	3,77,23,829	15,47,120	3,42,94,390
2029	3,96,75,251	16,55,419	3,60,68,410
2030	4,16,94,348	17,71,298	3,79,03,953
2031	4,37,78,965	18,95,289	3,97,99,059
2032	4,59,26,106	20,27,959	4,17,51,005
2033	4,81,31,808	21,69,917	4,37,56,190
2034	5,03,90,998	23,21,811	4,58,09,998
2035	5,26,97,326	24,84,337	4,79,06,660
2036	5,50,42,994	26,58,241	5,00,39,085
2037	5,74,18,543	28,44,318	5,21,98,676
2038	5,98,12,635	30,43,420	5,43,75,123

End of Year	Amount at end of Year	Expenses per Year	Balance after Expenses
2039	6,22,11,793	32,56,460	5,65,56,176
2040	6,46,00,120	34,84,412	5,87,27,382
2041	6,69,58,979	37,28,321	6,08,71,799
2042	6,92,66,644	39,89,303	6,29,69,676
2043	7,14,97,898	42,68,554	6,49,98,090
2044	7,36,23,600	45,67,353	6,69,30,545
2045	7,56,10,185	48,87,068	6,87,36,532
2046	7,74,19,125	52,29,162	7,03,81,023
2047	7,90,06,314	55,95,204	7,18,23,921
2048	8,03,21,390	59,86,868	7,30,19,445
2049	8,13,06,985	64,05,949	7,39,15,441
2050	8,18,97,882	68,54,365	7,44,52,620
2051	8,20,20,082	73,34,171	7,45,63,711
2052	8,15,89,771	78,47,563	7,41,72,519
2053	8,05,12,167	83,96,892	7,31,92,879
2054	7,86,80,241	89,84,675	7,15,27,492
2055	7,59,73,303	96,13,602	6,90,66,639
2056	7,22,55,424	1,02,86,554	6,56,86,749
2057	6,73,73,693	1,10,06,613	6,12,48,811
2058	6,11,56,278	1,17,77,076	5,55,96,617
2059	5,34,10,288	1,26,01,471	4,85,54,807
2060	4,39,19,385	1,34,83,574	3,99,26,714
2061	3,24,41,157	1,44,27,424	2,94,91,961
2062	1,87,04,195	1,54,37,344	1,70,03,813
2063	24,04,861	1,65,17,958	21,86,237

Fig 23: *Snapshot of nest egg calculator results*

A few points to be noted from the above results in Fig 23 from the nest egg calculator are:

1. The nest egg balance keeps increasing every year during the first half of your remaining life and goes from ₹ 1.65 Crores in 2014 to a peak of ₹ 8.2 Crores in 2051 (37 years). That's a good sign.

2. The nest egg balance drops drastically from ₹ 8.2 Crores in 2051 to ₹ 0.24 Crores in 2062 (11 years). This is less than what you started with. This is "inflation" at work.

3. Look at the expenses per year in 2063. It is 1.6 Crores per annum. It is 25 times the expenses you started with. That is "inflation" for you!!

4. If you live for another 1 or 2 years beyond the last expected year of life (2063), you will be completely bankrupt as your expenses are far higher than your nest egg balance in 2063.

5. It is therefore very important to arrive at a correct and safe nest egg balance which will last throughout your life. Remember that the earlier you retire, the longer you survive, and therefore, you will need a bigger nest egg balance.

6. To be on the safe side, we should start with a few more Lacs of rupees in the nest egg before we declare ourselves to be financially independent or try and control our expenses each month.

Going back to the inputs that we need to create a high level financial independence plan, we have got the first 2 inputs i.e., the starting point (today) as well as the end point (value of the amount in the nest egg once you declare yourself financially independent).

Next we have to know the time it will take to reach the end point from the starting point.

Duration to reach from the starting point to the end point

Once you know the starting point and the end point, you are in a position to calculate the approximate time period (number of years) you will need to reach your final goal and become financially independent.

The following factors influence the duration taken to reach your target nest egg:

1. Starting point
   a. You already have the starting point. This is the starting size of your nest egg today.

2. End point
   a. You just calculated the final size of the nest egg in the previous section.

3. Monthly savings
   a. This is the amount of monthly savings that you can manage today.
   b. This amount is added to your nest egg. This is the single most important factor for you to reach to your end point as fast as possible.
   c. This is calculated from the monthly cash outflow and inflow exercise that we did earlier.

4. Savings increment per year
   a. As you work through your job or your business, you need to estimate the approximate percentage increase in your income every year, due to salary increments, promotions, increased business revenue etc.

b. This increase in income contributes directly to your nest egg.

5. Return on investments

    a. This is the expected percentage return on investments made from your current nest egg.

    b. This also gets added to your starting point every year.

    c. You have already made an assumption of this number in the nest egg calculation.

Once you have these inputs available, calculating the duration to reach the end goal of financial freedom involves the following simple steps.

If you access the website and download the worksheet on "Duration Calculator", you need not bother about the process given below. However, it is worthwhile understanding how the calculations are done.

1. Take the starting point and calculate the interest earned on the starting point nest egg.

2. Calculate your savings for the year based on the monthly target savings.

3. Add both the above to the nest egg that you started with and accumulate by the end of the year.

4. The same exercise is repeated each year till you reach the end point accumulation of the nest egg.

Figure 24 on the facing page is a snapshot of the inputs needed to do the calculation using "duration calculator".

Input Description	Input Value	
Start Point	INR 40,00,000	Net Worth today
End Point	INR 1,75,00,000	
Monthly Savings	INR 2,00,000	Nest Egg Amount
Savings increment per year	10%	
ROI	10%	
Current Year	2011	

Fig 24: *Inputs for duration calculator*

Based on the above inputs, Fig 25 shows the expected output results of the duration calculator.

End of Year	Principal	Accrued Interest	Saving for the year	Total
2011	INR 40,00,000	INR 0	INR 24,00,000	INR 64,00,000
2012	INR 64,00,000	INR 0	INR 26,40,000	INR 90,40,000
2013	INR 90,40,000	INR 0	INR 29,04,000	INR 1,19,44,000
2014	INR 1,19,44,000	INR 0	INR 31,94,400	INR 1,51,38,400

Fig 25: *Duration calculator results*

It must be noted that if the nest egg at the starting point was 40 lacs, and your savings and ROI are as per the above inputs, it takes 4 years to reach the target nest egg of ₹ 1.75 Crores.

So, by the end of Step 3, our high level financial freedom plan is ready.

We now know:

1. Where we are today (Starting point or net worth)

2. Where we need to reach (Size of the nest egg)

3. How much time we would need to reach the end point (Duration)

It is now time to move to Step 4, in which these numbers are considered in detail on a monthly basis, so that you can track your plan more consistently.

If you have doubt regarding any of these three critical parameters i.e., starting point, end point and the duration, take time to revisit your calculations or re-adjust the numbers. These numbers are the most critical inputs to Step 4 and any error here will lead to an incorrect detailed financial freedom plan in Step 4. A strong foundation with the right numbers will help you obtain the correct results of your hard work.

Step 4: Create a detailed financial freedom plan

You know key numbers or the main milestones for your financial independence, namely:

1. Starting point (nest egg that you have today)

2. End point (final nest egg amount that can trigger your independence)

3. Duration (number of years) you will need to reach from the starting point to the end point.

Now it's time to create a detailed financial independence plan. This is a very important step in your journey to achieve financial independence. This is the plan that you will have to refer to almost 3-4 times a month and update it with the actual portfolio status.

It will be your friend through your journey and will force you to think of innovative ways to reach your monthly targets (if you lag behind at any stage).

The detailed financial plan starts with using the inputs from high level financial plan that we just created in Step 3.

At the bare minimum, you will need an Excel spreadsheet to start preparing and tracking your detailed financial plan. You could use some advanced tools as well but I have always believed that you should not be at the mercy of any tools to get started. Once you have started you can always improve and innovate as you become more adept at the process.

You need to track the parameters given below in your detailed financial independence plan. Initially it is enough that you understand the meaning and significance of the parameters and how they are calculated. Later on in the book a template will be given you can also download the template for your monthly tracking from the website.

1. Year and month
   a. At the minimum, we must have a target amount for the nest egg for every month i.e., how much we are going to accumulate in the nest egg by the end of each month.
   b. This can be typically achieved by taking the annual total target amount as calculated in Fig 25.

2. Planned nest egg amount at the end of each month
   a. Divide your total target annual amount for each year (derived from Fig 25) into monthly amounts.
   b. This could be an equal distribution across the year or vary depending on specific incomes/increases expected in the middle of the year. To start with, equal distribution throughout the year is fine.

3. Planned interest per month
   a. Once you have the cumulative monthly target nest egg amount planned, plan for the monthly returns that this nest egg can give you at that stage. (you can expect roughly 8 to 10% of your nest egg amount as returns on your investments).

b. This is an important number since this gives you the visibility to how close you are coming to the monthly expenses that you are targeting post your financial freedom.

4. Actual investments

   a. Split actual investments that you make every month on various debt and equity asset classes within your portfolio.

   b. Make sure you invest and track the actual investments on a monthly basis.

5. Actual total nest egg amount at the end of each month

   a. Total all the monthly investments in your portfolio to get the actual nest egg amount for each month.

6. Percentage achieved vs planned amount

   a. Comparing the actual nest egg amount with the planned nest egg amount for each month gives you an idea whether you are on track with your plan or not.

   b. If there is a negative deviation i.e., your actual investments are lower compared to whatever you planned, you may have to start thinking of innovative ways to get closer to the plan.

   c. If there is a positive deviation, your target date should start becoming nearer than the date you planned.

7. Total accumulated returns/interest

   a. Calculate the total actual accumulated return on investments as compared to the plan and see if you are ahead of the plan or not.

   b. For FDs, we can put the exact expected returns against the exact month of maturity while for other tools, we must take a defined percentage of the investment as the return. This percentage can be based on the returns given by the specific tool in the last few years.

8. Actual nest egg yield per month/royalty per month
   a. Calculate the actual yield per month to see if you are ahead of the planned yield per month.
   b. See that you are inching closer to meeting your monthly expenses that you have planned for.

Figure 26 is a snapshot of the detailed financial independence plan that I used to track my progress on a monthly basis. While this allows for monthly tracking, I would normally update this sheet at least 3-4 times a month and think of ways to earn more, save more, get innovative to earn and save… and make sure that not only do I stay with the plan but go much ahead of it. Figure 26 on the following page shows the status as on Oct 2011 (4.5 years after I started on my journey to financial freedom).

Let me try and explain the data in this important snapshot shown in Fig 26:

1. Column A : Month/Year (Yr 2011 expanded to show each month)

2. Column B : Planned nest egg for each month

3. Column C : Planned returns per month

4. Columns D to P : Actual investment breakup under various debt and equity tools in my portfolio

5. Column Q : Total actual nest egg accumulated at the end of each month

6. Column R : Percentage achieved (actual nest egg expressed as a percentage of the planned nest egg value). 100% indicates that the actual nest egg at the end of the month is the same as that which was planned for the same month

Month / Year	Planned Principal	Int/mn	HDFC FDs	ICICI FDs	Others	Rel. MF	FMPs	Stocks	IBM Stocks	PPF	EPF	Savings	Gratuity	SuperAnn	Gold	TOTAL	% Ach	Total Acc. Interest	Royalty pm
Y 2007	2,40,000	0	1,25,000	10,000		8,000		0	0	0	0					1,43,000	60	2,635	220
Y 2008	6,00,000	1,600	4,79,695	0		44,430		90,861		0	5,04,364			90,931		12,10,281	202	13,126	1,094
Y 2009	11,40,000	4,000	5,57,856	73,000		56,430		1,56,989		1,97,415	7,15,186			97,747		18,54,623	163	49,469	4,122
Y 2010	19,20,000	7,600	6,54,172	1,00,000	30,000	68,430		3,73,514		3,03,208	9,57,280			1,05,079	21,948	25,83,631	135	1,07,759	8,980
1	20,20,000		6,56,172	1,00,000	0	86,036	0	3,91,947		3,03,208	9,74,034			1,05,701	27,998	26,45,096	131	6392	
2	21,20,000		6,56,172	1,00,000	0	87,036	0	4,10,947		3,03,208	9,90,788			1,06,323	27,998	26,88,472	127		
3	22,20,000		6,56,172	1,00,000	0	88,036	0	4,16,947		3,03,208	10,07,542			1,06,945	27,998	27,06,848	122		
4	23,20,000		7,01,172	1,00,000	0	89,036	0	4,16,947		3,25,065	10,07,542	3,25,000		1,07,613	27,998	31,00,373	134	22123.30667	
5	24,20,000		7,16,172	1,00,000	0	90,036	0	4,27,945		3,25,065	10,07,542	3,05,000		1,08,281	36,948	31,16,989	129	11424	
6	25,20,000		8,86,172	1,00,000	0	91,036	0	4,27,945		3,95,065	10,07,542	1,68,000		1,08,949	46,310	32,31,019	128	10662	
7	26,20,000		9,85,172	1,00,000	0	92,036	0	4,65,594		3,95,065	10,07,542	1,84,000		1,09,617	46,310	33,85,336	129		
8	27,20,000		11,83,172	1,00,000	0	93,036	0	5,63,927		3,95,065	10,07,542	1,01,500		1,10,285	58,900	36,13,327	133		
9	28,20,000		12,82,172	1,00,000	0	1,14,036	0	6,11,240		3,95,065	10,07,542	2,17,810		1,10,953	10,000	38,48,818	136		
10	29,20,000		13,81,172	1,00,000	0	1,15,036	0	5,75,434	0	3,95,065	10,07,542	2,77,600		1,11,621	10,000	39,73,470	136		
11	30,20,000		13,81,172	2,84,000	0	1,16,036	25,000	6,71,389		3,95,065	10,07,542	1,26,250	1,43,923	1,12,289	10,000	42,72,666	141		
12	31,20,000		14,31,172	3,78,000	1,000	1,17,036	25,000	7,66,691		4,25,065	10,07,542	28,000	1,43,923	1,12,957	21,965	44,58,351	143		
Year 2011	31,20,000	12,800	14,31,172	3,78,000	1,000	1,17,036	25,000	7,66,691		4,25,065	10,07,542	28,000	1,43,923	1,12,957	21,965	44,58,351	143	2,66,282	22,190
Year 2012	49,20,000	20,800	17,85,172	5,62,943	1,000	30,500	25,000	0		5,56,205	12,88,862	8,98,098	1,43,923	1,20,973	1,91,847	56,04,523	114	3,05,100	25,425
Year 2013	76,80,000	32,800	17,85,172	5,62,943	1,000	42,500	25,000	0		5,56,205	15,49,838	8,98,098	1,43,923	1,28,989	1,91,847	58,85,515	77	5,60,904	46,742
Year 2014	1,18,80,000	51,200	17,85,172	5,62,943	1,000	54,500	25,000	0		5,56,205	18,10,814	8,98,098	1,43,923	1,37,005	1,91,847	61,66,507	52	2,61,863	21,822
Year 2015	1,78,80,000	79,200																	
Retirement Year 2016																		14,58,161	1,21,513

Fig 26: Snapshot of detailed financial independence plan

7. Column S : Actual returns as of end of year

8. Column T : Actual returns per month

We have now created a detailed financial independence plan with which we can track the following:

- ▶ What is my monthly target for the nest egg?
- ▶ Where have I reached compared to the target?
- ▶ How am I performing? Will I be financially free by the target date?
- ▶ What is my exact investment in each asset class of the portfolio?

Do not move ahead till you have created a detailed plan of your own.

Spend time here. If you use all the tools and templates that I have given you on the website, you should be able to create a detailed financial independence plan in less than one or two days.

A good start is half the battle won!

Step 5: Execute your financial freedom plan

If you have a solid, detailed and a realistic plan, you are off to a great start. Congratulations on reaching this milestone.

On the other hand, it is just the beginning, so do not get too complacent about it.

Whatever you have done until now was probably a onetime effort. Obviously, there may be times when you may have to tune your goals or timelines during your journey, but you will, never have to spend so much effort on planning again.

Most of your effort will now go in execution of the plan. This step is your daily bread and butter on what needs to be done every day to reach what you have planned.

I am going to share most of my own learning in this section. We will go through each investment tool under each asset class. This will help you align all your long-term goals in the plan with the investment tools to be used to achieve those goals.

Fixed deposits

The first and the most obvious tool that I started using was fixed deposits.

We have already seen that bank fixed deposits provide a better interest rate than money kept in your savings account.

The first recommendation that I have for all budding financially independent professionals is that make sure you have online banking enabled with your banker. It is not mandatory but it is highly advisable because soon you will have a large number of FDs which would be cumbersome to manage without online banking facilities. All you have to do is fill up a simple form to get your account enabled for online banking. It is a onetime effort but pays you 'n' number of times.

Remember the principle "Pay yourself first before you pay others" and make sure that with your next salary or next cash inflow, you make the first fixed deposit before starting to spend money on your other routine expenses.

Figure 27 is a snapshot from my tracker of the first few fixed deposits that I started with in the year 2007. You can see that I started off with only fixed deposits and that too of a small sum of ₹ 10,000/-. You can also see that I started moving ahead of my targets in the fourth month. This is the power of goals and of having a detailed month-wise plan. It can help you achieve what you could not have achieved otherwise. It will drive you to save money in ways you would never have thought possible.

"Month / Year"	Invested Amt			
	Planned		Actual	
	Principal	Int / mn	HDFC FDs	ICICI FDs
1	20,000		10,000	
2	40,000		40,000	
3	60,000		60,000	
4	80,000		1,05,000	
5	1,00,000		1,15,000	
6	1,20,000		1,25,000	
7	1,40,000		1,55,000	
8	1,60,000		1,91,000	

Fig 27: *Tracker snapshot of the first few months in 2007*

Bank fixed deposits are a great way to start your journey, mainly because the principal amount that you invested is assured and you know exactly what interest you will earn and when. This is not a trivial thing, because once you get into stocks, MFs, FMPs, you will realize how good it feels to have your principal amount and your returns assured. This does not mean that you should not invest in stocks or MFs or FMPs, but rather that it is always good to start on a relatively more assured footing.

Typically, bank fixed deposits should be around 15 to 20% of your portfolio when you become a mature investor. You can start off with even 100% of your portfolio being fixed deposits. It is more important to get into the habit of paying yourself first and starting the journey right now rather than anything else.

While creating your fixed deposits online, make sure to take care of the following points:

▶ Look for the best possible interest rates. As discussed in previous sections, most banks pay you higher rates for special periods. For example, a bank may pay 8.75% for a 1 year deposit and 9.25% for a 1 year and 16 day deposit.

We have already studied the reasons for this. Choose the best interest rate for the best period as suitable to you before locking your FD.

▶ While choosing the FD maturity option, look for a cumulative deposit option rather than an interest payout option. It is important to leverage the benefit of compounding interest. In an interest payout option, interest keeps coming back to you in quarterly or half yearly periods. This leads to interest not participating in cumulative growth and you have a higher probability of using the interest on "other unwanted expenses."

▶ I would advice not to choose to automatically renew the FD. Instead you should choose an option to transfer the matured amount back to your savings account. Do not worry. If you have online account, it just takes one or two minutes to create a new FD after logging into your account. There are various reasons for not going in for an automatically renewal facility.

    ➤ First and foremost, it feels good to see your money growing and flowing (with interest) from FDs back to your savings account. This feeling of money growing is a vital boost for your dream of financial freedom.

    ➤ You may want to change the period or amount of FD to get the maximum interest rate prevalent at the time of setting up the next FD. For example, a 1 year 16 day FD may have given you the maximum benefit last year but this year, it may be 2 years and 16 days or it may be 1 year and 20 days. If we automatically renew it, we will have no choice or control over the rate of interest.

    ➤ You may want to rotate your money across different investment tools in your portfolio depending on the market scenario. For example, if you feel that some stocks are really available at a good price and you have a rotating fund through FDs, it may be better to move the money in stocks or mutual funds and balance your portfolio.

➤ You could also utilize this opportunity to add some more "sundry money" to the matured amount and set up a new FD. For example, suppose a FD worth ₹ 10,000 matured and gave you Rs, 10,900. Then instead of renewing the FD at ₹ 10,900, it is better typically round it off to ₹ 11,000 and setup a new FD. These small amounts of money that you keep adding to each FD over and above the interest you accumulate get "really large" as we move along. The best part is that they do not affect your budget at all. You will see that you can still manage your expenses as you were doing earlier.

Another recommendation that I have for you as you become more and more mature in handling fixed deposits is to have online accounts from 2-3 different banks, with one of them at least being a public sector bank. I personally started with having online FDs with HDFC bank. After 8 months, I also started investing in ICICI bank and of late I have added State Bank of India as the public sector bank where I make my fixed deposits. The purpose is not to complicate things, but to make sure that:

▶ Not to put all your eggs in the same basket. Having all fixed deposits in one private sector bank may not be the best idea.

▶ Make use of the best interest rate available among all the banks. Different banks often change their rate of interest, offered to the consumers, depending on the economy and other market situations. It is beneficial to compare the interest rates offered by these banks and then pick the one which best suits you. You can transfer funds across banks and get the best possible interest rate available in the market.

A general thumb rule which I used was that whenever you see FD interest rates in the range of 9% to 10%, it is normally time to book FDs for longer tenures like 2-3 years and for anything less than 9%, it is best to book for 1 year so that you can have an option to look at the revised rates after 1 year and see if you can block your money for a higher period.

To understand and predict the FD interest rates, you will have to study the relation of FD interest rates with the repo rate or the base lending rates that the central bank like Reserve Bank of India keeps announcing. Normally, if you keep reading certain economic articles, you will come to know if the repo rate is likely to go up and down a few weeks/months in advance. FD rates normally go hand in hand with the repo rates. This gives you a fair idea whether you want to immediately go for the fixed deposit or wait for a few days/weeks to see if the banks change the FD rates on the higher side.

If you have a large number of bank fixed deposits, it is very important to keep a track of their maturity dates and the amounts. It is also important to store the FD receipts which are generated online. These receipts are either available online anytime when you login into your online bank account or are emailed to you within a day or two of FD creation. It is advisable to create a suitable folder on your computer/ laptop and keep a copy of these receipts with you for later reference.

To keep a track of all your FDs with their amounts and maturity dates, banks will normally give you an option to look at the summary of all your fixed deposits, which allows you to see the FD number, amount, rate of interest, maturity date, maturity amount etc.

Figure 28 on the following page shows a snapshot of the FD section of the tracker that I maintain for keeping a track of all my portfolio transactions.

Recurring deposits

Opening a bank Recurring Deposit (RD) is not very different from opening a fixed deposit. You can do it and track it online. Most of the points mentioned for FDs are also applicable for RDs.

Investing money in RDs can be a good second step in your plan execution when you are comfortable with tracking your fixed deposits online.

Since RDs are mostly invested in for a longer tenure as compared to FDs, you should invest when you feel that the rate of interest is relatively higher. Start with smaller amounts that are withdrawn automatically from your bank account.

After one or two years when you are more mature about saving money and do not need automatic deduction from your account, then RDs do not really give you any benefit over FDs.

But initially RDs are not a bad idea at all. I opened RDs twice before I decided that I could handle money myself.

Public provident fund

It is very important not to forget one of the most important traditional investment tools. If you do not have a PPF account after 6 months of starting your investment plan, you are missing out on this tool. In fact, if you open this account from Day 1 of your journey, you will never regret your decision.

The process to open the account as well as the advantages offered by a PPF account, have been documented in the previous section. Practices based on my experience are given below.

- ▶ The financial year in India starts on 1st April. Invest, if you can, to the maximum limit allowed in a PPF account within

Invest-ment ID	Tool	Agency	Investment Number	Invested	Investment	Maturity Amount	Maturity Date	No. of Stocks	Status	Rate of Return
27	FD	HDFC Bank	FD_1294470229087	25,000	27-May-11	30,139	10-Jun-13	NA	Invested	10.08%
28	FD	HDFC Bank	FD_1294470230896	5,000	13-Jun-11	6,028	27-Jun-13	NA	Invested	10.08%
29	FD	HDFC Bank	FD_1375447003621	50,000	13-Jun-11	60,278	27-Jun-13	NA	Invested	10.08%
30	FD	HDFC Bank	FD_1338447000863O	45,000	16-Jun-11	54,250	30-Jun-13	NA	Invested	10.08%
31	FD	HDFC Bank	FD_1375447003372A	95,000	21-Jun-11	1,14,528	05-Jul-13	NA	Invested	10.08%
32	FD	HDFC Bank	FD_1375447003392A	45,000	30-Jun-11	54,250	14-Jul-13	NA	Invested	10.08%
33	FD	HDFC Bank	FD_1375447003438A	99,000	20-Jul-11	1,19,350	03-Aug-13	NA	Invested	10.08%
34	FD	HDFC Bank	FD_1375447003462A	99,000	05-Aug-11	1,19,350	19-Aug-13	NA	Invested	10.08%
35	FD	HDFC Bank	FD_1375447003486S	99,000	25-Aug-11	1,19,350	08-Sep-13	NA	Invested	10.08%
36	FD	HDFC Bank	FD_1375447003539A	99,000	2-Sep-11	1,19,350	08-Oct-13	NA	Invested	10.05%
141	FD	ICICI Bank	00711412807A	30,000	04-Feb-10	34,863	04-Apr-12	NA	Matured	7.50%
142	FD	ICICI Bank	007114130659	15,000	07-May-10	17,428	05-Jul-12	NA	Matured	7.49%
143	FD	ICICI Bank	007114130980	55,000	15-May-10	63,903	13-Jul-12	NA	Matured	7.49%
147	FD	HDFC Bank	FD_1294470241205	99,000	12-Oct-11	1,19,350	28-Oct-13	NA	Invested	10.05%
148	FD	ICICI Bank	007114147249	45,000	24-Oct-11	54,839	22-Dec-13	NA	Invested	10.11%
149	FD	ICICI Bank	00711414727A	45,000	25-Oct-11	54,839	23-Dec-13	NA	Invested	10.11%
150	FD	ICICI Bank	007114147317	45,000	28-Oct-11	52,165	09-Jun-13	NA	Invested	9.86%
151	FD	HDFC Bank	FD_1294470243738	7,002	19-Nov-11	8,441	05-Dec-13	NA	Invested	10.05%
152	FD	HDFC Bank	FD_2934830000907	12,807	17-Jan-11	13,908	02-Feb-12	NA	Matured	8.25%
153	FD	HDFC Bank	FD_2934830001296	12,707	18-Apr-11	13,837	03-May-12	NA	Matured	8.53%
154	FD	HDFC Bank	FD_2934830004543	5,734	23-Jun-11	6,223	07-Aug-12	NA	Matured	7.60%
155	FD	HDFC Bank	FD_1067447001842A	8,501	20-Aug-10	9,896	11-Sep-12	NA	Matured	7.96%
179	FD	ICICI Bank	FD_007114148036	49,000	24-Nov-11	56,817	07-Jul-13	NA	Invested	9.86%
188	FD	ICICI Bank	FD_007114148444	49,000	09-Dec-11	56,802	21-Jul-13	NA	Invested	9.86%
196	FD	ICICI Bank	FD_007114148732	45,000	20-Dec-11	52,165	01-Aug-13	NA	Invested	9.86%
197	FD	State Bank of India	FD_41682484	1,000	20-Dec-11	1,165	19-Sep-13	NA	Invested	9.43%
201	FD	HDFC Bank	FD_1375447003725A	50,000	29-Dec-11	55,010	14-Jan-13	NA	Invested	9.58%

Fig 28: Fixed deposit snapshot of my asset tracker

the first week or the first month, whichever is feasible in your case.

▶ As of writing this book, the limit of investment in a PPF account is ₹ 100,000 per financial year. Make sure you complete this quota before investing in any new FDs, RDs or any other tool.

▶ Most banks today that offer you a PPF account also offer the same facility online if you have a savings account with the same bank. I maintain a savings and a PPF account with the State Bank of India.

▶ Since you cannot transfer funds to your PPF account directly from any other bank, it makes sense to have a savings account with an online facility and a PPF account with the same bank/branch. Once you have this arrangement, it is easy to transfer funds from any bank to your bank's savings account and then to your PPF account.

▶ Never take the money out of PPF account till you are at least financially free, though the bank will allow you to withdraw funds after 5 years. In fact, you should never take money from your nest egg (any investment tool or asset class) till you attain financial freedom! That is where the power of compounding interest can be realized; otherwise you will always be caught up in this race of income and expenses.

▶ Figure 29 shows the snapshot of my PPF investments and its progress over time. Though I had a PF account since the last 15 years, I understood the real power of compounding only during this journey. You will therefore see a sudden jump in the total amount in the PPF account in 2010. This jump will be much larger in the coming few years because of the super power of compounding.

	PPF
Y 2007	0
Y 2008	0
Y 2009	1,97,415
Y 2010	3,03,208
Y 2011	4,25,065

Fig 29: *PPF Balance as on year end*

Retirement benefits (EPF/Gratuity/Superannuation)

You should continue to invest in all possible retirement benefits as per the policies of the company that you work with. Just make sure that you do not repeat the same mistakes as I did when I moved across companies.

Make sure you transfer the money to your new organization's PF office or EPFO by filling in the correct forms at the correct time. Never withdraw the PF funds. I made this mistake more than once before I realized that not only did I pay tax on the money I withdrew but soon spent the money in hand. I lost all benefits of compounding as well as the principle amount itself.

A word of caution on gratuity benefits — if you have worked with any organization for 3-4 years, see that you carry out all the calculations necessary regarding your gratuity benefits before you leave that organization. You will get gratuity benefits if you serve for a minimum of 5 years, and the gratuity amount is not a small amount by any means. Remember that once you move to a new organization, you have to prove yourself once again, and this takes at least 6 – 12 months. So, unless, there is a drastic change in your salary (e.g., it is doubled), it does not make sense to change jobs before completing at least 5 years.

Mutual funds

If you have never dealt with stocks before, mutual funds are the place to start. Some of my recommendations regarding mutual fund investments are

- Start investing in mutual funds within 12 months of the start of your journey.

- Make sure you have an online account so that you can track the status in real time. Today, you can open mutual fund accounts online if you have a valid PAN number[88] and the PAN number is registered with Know Your Customer (KYC[89]) office. When I started with Reliance Mutual Funds, I had to fill in forms manually, but now I can create online mutual fund accounts with UTI Mutual Funds and other mutual fund companies as well.

- Start investing in mutual funds with a small monthly Systematic Investment Plan[24] (SIP) and continue this way for about 12 months. I started off with ₹ 1000/- monthly SIP investments with Reliance mutual funds.

- This is the first time you might feel excited about the returns, which can be 40 to 50% in a year (I have realized even 1000% returns! No, this is not a mistake!) or you may realize that your money actually gave you negative returns in a specific time period. You must get used to either feeling. This will set some long-term perspectives in your mind. In the long run, you are more likely to win in the equity market since your fund is professionally managed in mutual funds. You will learn to cope with the day to day ups and downs of the markets and the mutual funds.

- While investing in mutual funds try and see that you start investing in funds with either a great track record or with funds in upcoming industries. I invested in Pharma based mutual funds as I realized the upside potential in this industry.

▶ After 12 months of investing in a specific mutual fund and tracking the ups and downs, you may want to buy more of the same or different funds from the same company. Normally, companies like Reliance and UTI will provide you with an online user id and password to their MF portal and then you can buy or sell any kind of funds from their sites.

▶ Your mutual fund account or portfolio number is linked to your bank account. Please make sure that you keep the linked bank account active.

▶ It is also advisable to try and see a few units on and off to see how money comes back to your linked accounts

▶ Many times, mutual funds will provide you with a debit card and make you feel that your mutual fund account is like a normal savings account. I recommend never keeping that debit card in your wallet. You can store it in a safe place in your home, in case you need it in an emergency.

▶ Mutual funds charge a significant entry fee with every investment that you make, so make sure that you do not use the mutual fund account as a savings account. You will never realize that you have paid a lot of money carrying out these transactions.

▶ Personally, I have continued my small SIP investments in mutual funds till date and buy over and above these SIP instalments on and off whenever I see an opportunity. Mutual funds can be your focus of attention for 12 to 24 months as far as the equity part of your portfolio is concerned but I do not recommend mutual funds in the long run i.e., when you have understood the market and have a better feel for what is happening around you and why. At that stage (which is around 24 months from the start of your journey), you must be an active player in stocks.

Gold

All of you must have dealt with gold at some stage of your life. I have also dealt with gold, but mainly see it once a year in my bank locker. It has become more of a liability of late since I have to pay locker rentals to the bank where I keep the gold in safe custody.

My views on gold have changed a lot during my journey towards financial freedom, as I saw its price fluctuating daily in the market.

Here are my recommendations on gold as an investment tool:

▶ Gold is not only a more secure investment than mutual funds but also a better performer, if you use it the way I am going to tell you. You should start investing in gold at the same time as you start in mutual funds i.e., within 9-12 months of starting your journey.

▶ First of all, you should completely forget physical gold as any kind of useful investment tool. Physical gold only has ornamental value and in today's world of artificial jewellery, I do not give too much significance to keeping gold as an ornament.

▶ You need to purchase gold ETFs. For this, as you have already seen, you will need to open a Demat account.

▶ Once you have a demat account, start buying 1 or 2 units of any of the gold ETFs at regular intervals or at dips. I have personally invested in HDFC gold ETFs and Goldman

Sachs Gold Funds. You can buy 1 or 2 units of them or any other gold ETFs that you may want to.

▶ I read lot of articles and advice from multiple sources that guided me to keep investing in gold at regular intervals and then stay invested because gold in your portfolio is a hedge against inflation. Its price will always increase with inflation and will keep you at par with the depreciated value of money based on inflation. This made a lot of sense to me and I continued investing in gold for 12-18 months.

▶ After about 40 months on my journey, I could relate rough patterns in gold price trends. Gold prices also have their own significant peaks and troughs if you ignore the day to day price fluctuations. In the long run (spanning 3-4 years), gold has always stayed at par with inflation, but careful study of short-term patterns i.e., over a few months, is very interesting. Once you understand those patterns, you can utilize them to your advantage to maximize your returns from gold.

▶ I have realized that it is almost always worth buying gold on dips. If the gold price has come down by more than 5%-7% of the average cost price at which you are holding the gold ETFs, it is almost always worthwhile to buy more. This is unlike the case of stocks where the stock price depends on the performance of the company whose stocks you are holding. To me, gold is much more predictable and I am assured that in the long run, it will give me returns which are at least equal to the rate of inflation.

▶ Gold prices normally fluctuate inversely as compared to the overall economic outlook and stock prices. The reasons for this are not difficult to understand at all. Once you have experienced this and seen it for yourself, it becomes much easier to take decisions regarding buying and selling gold. This is not an iron clad rule but I have found it to be mostly true in my experience. You must take an informed decision after you have seen and experienced this. 2011 was one of the toughest years for the world economy with the economic slowdown in the US and China, the Euro-zone crisis, high inflation and rupee depreciation in India. Due to all these factors, I realized stock returns of just 5.7% in 2011 but at the same time, my knowledge on gold and its correlation with stocks allowed me to reap and realize returns from gold investments of more than 56%!. This proves the value of diversification.

▶ Of late, I have removed all my gold from the bank locker and invested it more wisely in Gold Exchange Traded Funds[55] (ETFs), thus utilizing the peaks and troughs in gold prices. It was not an easy decision considering the conventional way of thinking in our families. I had to face stiff resistance with arguments like 'we will need this jewellery when our daughters get married' or 'we might need this for a rainy day' etc. I do not know how the marriage of the next generation will be celebrated and whether they will want to wear jewellery of older designs. I will need gold at that stage and I will be happy to buy what is needed for the marriage at the right time. Regarding a 'rainy day', well, that is what financial freedom is all about. Having said that, I do not want to force you into such decisions. First you should be convinced and invest small amounts of money. Once you have understood what is happening around you and understand the macro economy, you can think of such decisions but definitely not in the first 36 months of your journey.

Stocks

Stocks are the most feared and also the most profitable investment vehicle. I always believe in the age old saying that 'knowledge removes fear'. The more you understand stocks, the more enthusiastic you will be about them and more profit you will reap from them.

- ▶ First ground rule – Do not ever invest in stocks because someone has told you to do so. I have burnt my fingers enough times. Therefore I have the nerve to call this statement a rule (with no exception).

- ▶ My recommendation would be that you wait for at least 18-24 months in your journey before starting to invest in stocks or until you have at least 12 months experience in investing and tracking your mutual fund portfolio. It is important to understand the ups and downs of a stock based investment either directly through stocks or through mutual funds.

- ▶ You will need a securities online account to transact in stocks. If you are already trading in gold ETFs, you will already have such an account.

- ▶ To start with, you should not pick more than one or two stocks. Now the question is what kind of stock and what stocks? In general, the thumb rule is that blue chip companies pose less risk (and relatively lesser growth as well), and are good to start your stock portfolio with. I remember having started with a ₹ 5,000/ investment in ICICI Bank stock. I was fortunate to earn a 15% growth within 1 month. Even if you do not reap that kind of growth, at least you are sure that you will not lose your money in the long run.

- ▶ Another factor that I did not keep in mind for a long time during my journey was to make sure that I purchased stocks that can provide cash flow rather than only capital gains. I benefitted early in my journey and I depended a lot on various stock pick options that I subscribed for. When the market was on the upward trend, most of these stock pick suggestions turned out to be correct and I still remember times when the recommended stocks rose 15 to 20% in a single day. While such a handsome return so fast in the cycle can lead you to investing a disproportionate amount of money in stocks, very soon I realized that these stock pick recommendations do not always hold good, and in situations when they do not hold good, you do not know what to do with what you have bought. This situation mainly arose because I neither studied the stocks I was buying nor did I buy blue chip stocks which can give dividend cash flow. I did profit from a few of those stocks by making use of the dollar cost averaging principle but I am stuck with many of them even today.

▶ After this experience of blocked stocks and seeing a long downtrend in the market, I realized the hard way, what I read in Robert Kiyosaki's book, that we should always invest for cash flow rather than capital gains. Well, the fact remains that I had read this much earlier but one does not understand till one actually goes through the experience oneself. I put my mistakes behind me, but made sure I did not repeat the same mistakes. After this experience, I made sure that my future investments were mainly targeted towards cash flow generating blue chip stocks.

▶ You must do your own research to decide which dividend yielding stocks you should invest in. It is very easy to get the information on dividends distributed by any company over the last few years. You can simply go to stock exchange websites of the National Stock Exchange (NSE) (http://nseindia.com/) or the Bombay Stock Exchange (BSE) (http://bseindia.com/) and search for a specific company to get all the details about the company including the dividend amounts and the ex-dividend dates, at least for the last 5 years. Remember the importance of 'ex-dividend date' if you are investing for dividends.

▶ I did a comparative analysis on my equity portfolio by collecting some basic information around the dividend yield and the ex dividend date. This analysis allowed me to invest in good dividend yielding stocks on dips, thus making use of the concept of dollar cost averaging for high capital gains as well as good cash flow because of high dividends.

▶ Figure 30 on the following page shows a comparative analysis that I made for my portfolio. I learnt the hard way. Earlier, I invested mainly in stocks which did not pay any dividend at all. After all my experience, I have learnt and have started driving my portfolio towards high dividend yielding stocks.

▶ It is a onetime effort to collect these data, in case you have not done it to date. If you are a beginner in stocks, it is highly recommended to start this exercise from Day 1.

▶ While it is advisable to invest into mainly dividend yielding stocks till you become financially free and are in a position to take bigger risks, you should not forget that these dividend yielding stocks can yield handsome capital gains as well. You should never forget the potential of dollar cost averaging in giving you handsome capital gains along with dividends. Keep investing in such stocks on dips.

▶ Below is a real life example of dollar cost averaging from my actual stock portfolio for Suzlon Energy. The difference in this example as compared to that of K S Oils given earlier, is that this is a long-term investment (spanning across many years). This investment has not yielded its results at the time of writing this book, but it is just about to break free with one or two peak market days.

The price of this stock has been coming down for the last 2 years with the general fall of the market. Remember that we need to be careful that there are no other specific reasons for the stock price to come down. If that is the case, then it makes sense to utilize the power of dollar cost averaging.

Figure 31 shows an actual screenshot of the purchase history of Suzlon Energy stock that I still hold.

At the time of writing this book, I had still not sold the stock as it had not yet jumped above the current average cost. I am continuing to invest during dips to bring the average cost as low as possible since I am confident of the organization as such as well as being upbeat about the future of the industry (non conventional energy sources) to which Suzlon belongs.

One of the fundamental premises is that a corporate dealing with 'non conventional energy sources' is likely to have a better long-term future because of increased dependency on such sources of energy in the future.

Stock Name	Avg Buy Price	Active No. of shares	Next Dividend On	Dividend per share	Historical Dividend Yield	Total Dividend Expected	Active Invested Amount	Current Dividend Yield
Ashok Leyland	25.81	1546	Jun-12	1	3.87%	1546	39,900	3.87%
Ballarpur Industries	26.80	2747	Dec-12	0.6	2.24%	1648	73,625	2.24%
Bank Of Baroda	719.33	50	Jun-12	17	2.36%	850	35,308	2.41%
Bharti Airtel	377.49	39	Aug-12	1	0.26%	39	14,722	0.26%
Blue Star	185.60	54	Jul-12	1	0.54%	54	10,022	0.54%
Deepak Fertilizers	150.39	561	Jul-12	5.5	3.66%	3086	84,371	3.66%
DLF Ltd	240.45	163	Jul-12	2	0.83%	326	39,193	0.83%
GAIL India	378.39	41	Aug-12	6	1.59%	246	15,514	1.59%
GMR Infrastructure	48.68	1785	Aug-12	0	0.00%	0	86,894	0.00%
Kingfisher Airlines	21.87	960	Jun-12	0	0.00%	0	20,160	0.00%
MTNL	58.15	100	Jun-12	0	0.00%	0	5,815	0.00%
Noida Toll Bridge	28.01	2314	Oct-12	0.5	1.79%	1157	64,812	1.79%
Pantaloon Retail	218.29	54	Aug-12	0	0.00%	0	10,089	0.00%
Petronet LNG	157.27	160	Jul-11	2.5	1.59%	400	25,120	1.59%
Ranbaxy Laborataries	537.21	29	May-12	2	0.37%	58	15,579	0.37%
Reliance Power	139.28	145	Jul-12	0	0.00%	0	20,196	0.00%
SAIL	187.73	237	Jul-12	1.3	0.69%	308	44,492	0.69%
Shipping Corporation	66.96	597	Sep-12	3	4.48%	1791	39,978	4.48%
Shree Renuka Sugar	34.86	930	Oct-12	1	2.87%	930	32,418	2.87%
SJVN	20.00	5000		0.94	4.70%	4700	1,00,000	4.70%
SBI	1623.00	10	May-12	30	1.85%	300	21,526	1.39%
Suzlon	36.45	6243	Jul-12	0	0.00%	0	2,27,541	0.00%
Tata Chemicals	355.50	43	Jul-12	10	2.81%	430	15,287	2.81%
Tata Motors	263.92	116	Jun-12	4	1.52%	464	30,391	1.53%
Tulip Telecom	201.00	125	Aug-12	0	0.00%	0	25,125	0.00%
TVS Motors	43.75	619	Jan-12	0.7	1.60%	433	25,090	1.73%
Varun Shipping	18.89	1333	Jul-12	0.8	4.24%	1066	25,178	4.24%

Fig 30: *Equity portfolio analysis with dividend yields*

SUZLON ENERGY

HSL: SUZLTD | BSE Code : 532667 | NSE Symbol :SUZLON | ISIN: INE040H01021

TRANSACTIONS HISTORY

Date	Buy / Sell	Exchange	Qty.	Unit Price	Trans. Amount	Type
29-06-2009	Buy	NSE	1,424	63.84	90,908.16	Delivery
01-09-2010	Buy	NSE	195	46.50	9,067.50	Delivery
07-02-2011	Buy	BSE	104	47.05	4,893.20	Delivery
24-02-2011	Buy	BSE	112	44.35	4,967.20	Delivery
07-08-2011	Buy	BSE	210	46.60	9,786.00	Delivery
09-08-2011	Buy	BSE	245	42.20	10,339.00	Delivery
16-08-2011	Buy	BSE	250	38.25	9,562.50	Delivery

Fig 31: *Dollar cost averaging for Suzlon Energy*

Note that I have been continuously investing small amounts on dips in this stock, trying to utilize the concept of dollar cost averaging.

Figure 32 shows the calculation summary of the average cost of the stock due to dollar cost averaging.

Date	Trx Type	Exchange	Quantity	Unit Price	Amount	"Average Cost (Dollar Cost Averaging)"
29-Jun-09	Buy	NSE	1,424	63.84	90,908.16	63.84
1-Sep-10	Buy	NSE	195	46.5	9,067.50	61.75
7-Feb-11	Buy	BSE	104	47.05	4,893.20	60.86
24-Feb-11	Buy	BSE	112	44.35	4,967.20	59.86
7-Aug-11	Buy	BSE	210	46.6	9,786.00	58.49
9-Aug-11	Buy	BSE	245	42.2	10,339.00	56.75
16-Aug-11	Buy	BSE	250	38.25	9,562.50	54.93
Total			2,540		1,39,523.56	

Fig 32: *Dollar cost averaging for Suzlon Energy*

You can see from the above table that as I kept investing during stock dips, the average price of the stock that I held kept coming down.

As seen in the example, it came down from ₹ 63.84 in June 2009 to ₹ 54.93 in Aug 2011. Now, when the market goes up (and hopefully the stock as well), I will be in a better shape to sell the total stock holding with maximum profit. Let us assume that the market bounces back and the stock also bounces back to a level of ₹ 70 after a few months. While it is not a big jump from ₹ 63.84 to ₹ 70 in almost 2.5 years, let us consider the returns calculation in both the different cases i.e., the returns with and without dollar cost averaging.

Case 1 is if you invested in June 2009 and waited for the stock to go up to realize the capital gains, and Case 2 is if you invested during the recession downtime phase and are ready to sell the stock now, after understanding and utilizing the power of dollar cost averaging.

Case 1 (One time purchase)

June 2009

Unit cost of the stock	: ₹ 63.84
Stock units	: 1424
Invested amount	: 1424*63.84 = ₹ 90908.

Dec 2011

Unit price of the stock	: ₹ 70.00
Stock units held	: 1424
Realized amount	: 1424*70 = ₹ 99680
Profit	: 99680 – 90908 = ₹ 8772
Annualized returns	: 3.5%

Case 2 (With dollar cost averaging)

June 2009

Unit cost of the stock	: ₹ 63.84
Stock units	: 1,424
Invested amount	: 1,424*63.84 = ₹ 90,908.
Dollar cost investments	: 139,523

Dec 2011

Unit price of the stock	: ₹ 64.00
Stock units held	: 2,540
Realized amount	: 2,540*70 = ₹ 177,800
Profit	: 177,800 – 139,523 = ₹ 38,277
Annualized returns	: 10.6%

Remember that since your investments in Case 2 were over different time durations, the annualized returns will be calculated using the IRR formula as described earlier in the book. Figure 33 shows a snapshot of the IRR calculation in this case.

Year	Investment
2009	-90908
2010	-9067
2011	-39548
Dec 2011 Value	177800
IRR	10.6%

Fig 33: IRR/CAGR for Case 2 for Suzlon Energy

So, you can see the difference and power of this concept of dollar cost averaging.

You get approx 300% more returns (10.6% as compared to 3.5%) on your invested amount just by using the simple concept of dollar cost averaging.

Real estate

This is the big league investment. My personal recommendation for each one of you would be to wait for at least 40-50 months after you start your journey before you enter this league of investors. Remember, we are talking about real estate as an investment and not about the house you live in.

Once you are comfortably placed financially and are closer to your financial freedom goal, this is one of the investment tools which will give you the biggest returns. We have already seen that real estate investments yield the maximum returns because they leverage the bank's investment on the loaned amount along with your own investment.

But since this investment involves a huge amount of money, it is recommended to be kept for the last leg of your financial freedom journey or after you have achieved financial freedom.

Follow the recommendations already provided under the section on investment tools to take a call on the real estate you want to invest in.

I fortunately bought some real estate in 2004 which appreciated to 5 times its price by 2010. But my recommendation is to delay using this investment tool till the last leg of the financial freedom journey, unless you have prior exposure and are already comfortable in this asset class.

Step 6: Track your financial freedom plan

As important as it is to track the planned vs actual nest egg on a regular basis as shown in the spreadsheet in Fig 26, it is equally important to monitor and track the portfolio through multiple metrics and dashboards

Dashboards provide you with a pictorial presentation of the facts which are not only easier to absorb and help in faster decision making, but are also capable of forecasting based on the existing trend of planned vs actual investments to date.

I have listed some of the dashboards that I used while tracking my financial progress, below. These will be useful for you as well. Remember to use what you think will work for you. It is not mandatory to use all of them. However, in general, each of the dashboards described here have a specific purpose and objective.

Let us start looking at these charts and dashboards one by one.

Executive portfolio summary

This first dashboard provides you with the most rudimentary information that you need as you start building your nest egg. It tells how your portfolio is divided amongst the various debt and equity investments that you have made.

Based on various thumb rules and the risk-reward strategy that you may be using for building your portfolio, you may want to alter the portfolio distribution as you go along or ensure you stick to the same portfolio.

Figure 34 shows the executive portfolio summary for my portfolio as on October 2011 – during my journey towards financial freedom.

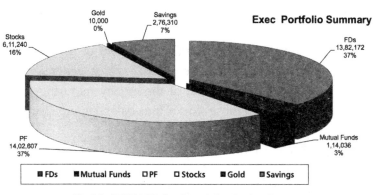

Fig 34: *IRR/CAGR for Case 2 for Suzlon Energy*

Let us understand what the executive portfolio summary from Fig 34 can tell us about my investment profile. As I have mentioned, there is a purpose for each dashboard, so let us see some of the immediate conclusions that you can draw from this dashboard:

1. It tells me clearly that my investment in stocks is about 16% of my portfolio (you can count it as 19% if you include mutual funds as well). The general thumb rule that we have studied earlier says that it should be (100-your age)% which should be ideally around 62%. So, instantly I know that I am way behind in stock investments and my current portfolio is a very conservative one.

2. The debt portion of my portfolio is extraordinarily high. Look at the amount of money in FDs and PF (almost 74%). Although, this is fine for the first 18-24 months of your journey, you need to start taking more risks and balance your portfolio, as you go along.

3. The commodities (gold in this case) portion is significantly lower than the general thumb rule of 5-10%.

This kind of dashboard view, therefore, gives me a real time perspective of my current portfolio allocation and therefore helps me in future alignment and adjustment of my portfolio. So, I should look at "attractive stocks" which generate good dividends and re-allocate some of the money maturing out of the next FD into one of those stocks, thus balancing my portfolio.

Monthly returns – Planned vs actual

This dashboard tracks your actual returns per month (on a yearly basis) as compared to the planned returns per month (again on a yearly basis).

Figure 35 on the following page shows a snapshot in time of the monthly returns dashboard for my portfolio. You can see that I was well ahead of the plan on a year to year basis.

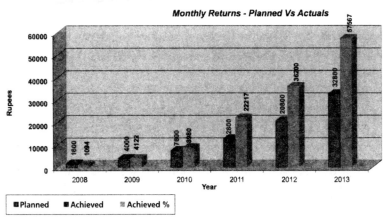

Fig 35: *Monthly returns – Planned vs actuals*

As the actual returns get closer to your monthly expenses, you start feeling comfortable that you are inching closer to your target. Your nest egg now grows exponentially if you do not touch the returns as of now.

The dashboard in Fig 35 also shows that I was well ahead of my planned monthly returns on a year to year basis, and hence on course with my financial freedom plan.

Percentage achieved vs planned (for the last 12 months)

This dashboard shows where you stand on a monthly basis, as compared to your planned nest egg amount for each month. Figure 36 on the following page shows you the percentage achieved vs planned dashboard for my portfolio.

Any percentage above 100 ensures that you are ahead of the target amount in your nest egg amount at a particular time. The trend shows how you have been performing for the last 12 months.

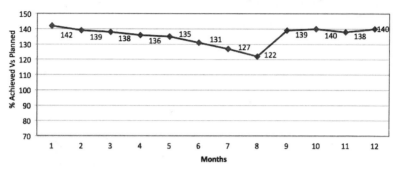

Fig 36: *Percentage achieved vs planned*

Figure 36 shows that I was around 40% ahead of the plan as far as the nest egg amount was concerned as compared to the total target for a particular month.

Nest egg (actual and forecast)

This dashboard in the graph of Fig 37 on the following page shows the accumulated nest egg amount over a period of time.

Note that I have a line on this graph showing the trend of my nest accumulation over the next 3-4 years.

You will notice that the nest egg tends to grow very fast in the later years – indicating the immense power of compounded interest.

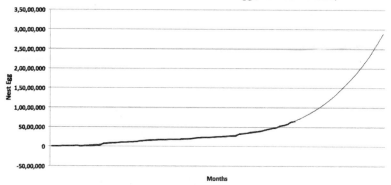

Fig 37: *Nest egg (actual and forecast)*

The above graph shows two different lines:

1. The bold line shows the actual savings accumulated over several months.

2. The dotted black line, which is a projection of the bold blue line as it would look for accumulating a nest egg of approx ₹ 20 million.

3. Note that, as the trend predicts, it takes less than 25% of the time to cover the last 75% of the journey. This is the power of compounding interest.

4. This shows that we need to be very patient on this journey. At times, we might get impatient and feel that we are not saving enough, but since compound interest has a delayed gratification, it will take its time. Patience will pay.

In case you are overwhelmed by charts and graphs and are thinking that you will not be able to produce them in your case, I have provided you with sample financial planning sheets along with linked charts. These charts are created automatically once you fill your data in the financial planning sheets. You are free to download these sheets and charts from the website http://www.ratrace2freedom.com

Happy tracking!

Step 7: Tune your portfolio for the coming year

When I was in software industry, we used to follow a very important method to ensure that we were able to analyze the existing trends and continue to improve continuously as we went along.

This methodology is better known as "Pareto Analysis". What it essentially says is that if you look at the defects in any software, and categorize these defects by the causes of the defects and draw a category wise chart, you will realize that 80% of the defects are caused by 20% of the causes. Once you have carried out this analysis, you need to go back and address those causes (20%) before you fix the defects so that most of the defects (80%) can be avoided in the future.

This method of analysis is very well proven and a de-facto standard in the software industry throughout the world. The same concept can and must be applied in other spheres of life. You will see the same concept in your office or your area of work. 20% of the people around will do 80% of the work. When the base lending rate goes up, you earn more interest in FDs, conversely, your rate of interest in FDs reduces when the base lending rate goes down. The same principle applies when we talk about money. 20% of the people across the globe hold more than 80% of the money.

The same rule can also be applied to decide the investments you make in a particular year before you go on to continue investing next year.

It is important to understand what returns each of your investment tools gave you in a defined period of time before continuing to invest with the same portfolio breakup or deciding to change the portfolio distribution. We have already studied various formulae for calculating these returns in the early chapters of this book. Now is the time to put those formulae into practice to decide which investment is giving you better returns and which is not.

When I did this analysis on my portfolio for the first time and saw the results, I was in for a few surprises. This is precisely what is going to happen with you as well if you devote enough time to this analysis.

Figure 38 on the following page shows the results of the first such analysis I carried out. I was always under the impression that fixed deposits and stocks were giving me good returns (because I could see the money coming each year), what I never realized was that gold ETFs and mutual funds were giving me better results than fixed deposits.

Once I understood the relative position of returns from multiple investment sources and asset classes, I was in a better position to decide where my focus should be for the next year.

Based on the above analysis, I formulated the investment strategy for the next year. It was a simple but very important step. Many of us continue to invest without tuning our investments to get better results.

I started ranking my returns on investments and then formulated the ranking for the coming year (i.e., the priority of each investment I should make to move forward). Figure 39 shows the ranking of all my asset classes based on the returns that I received in a specific year.

Mutual Funds		Fixed Deposits	
Investment		Investment	
Year	Amount	Year	Return %
2007	-6,000	2007	8.00
2008	-20,000	2008	8.25
2009	-30,000	2009	8.55
2010	-12,000	2010	7.75
2011		2011	7.20
Value as on Dec 2010	1,01,800	2012	7.21
IRR	18.66%	Avg Ann ROI	7.83%

Gold		Provident Fund (EPF + PPF)	
Investment		Investment	
Year	Amount	Year	Return %
2010	-21,948	EPF	8.50
2011		PPF	8.00
Value as on Dec 2010	24,118		
IRR	9.89%	Avg Ann ROI	8.25%

Stocks	
Investment	
Year	Amount
2008	-67,861
2009	-33,931
2010	-1,52,688
2011	
Invested Value as on Dec 2010	3,74,500
IRR	24.65%

Fig 38: *Calculation of returns*

ROI vs Investment			
Financial Tool	Ann. ROI	ROI Rank	Inv Rank
MFs	18.66%	2	4
FDs	7.83%	5	2
Gold	9.89%	3	5
PF	8.25%	4	1
Stocks	24.65%	1	3

Fig 39: *Ranking table for returns*

Once I had the investment ranking for the coming year, it was much easier to decide how my investments should be broken up for the coming year. Figure 40 shows the guiding principles for investments in the coming year based on the ranking table.

Investment Focus in 2011 (based on ROI vs Investment till date)	
Mutual Funds	Massive investment needed
FDs	No new FDs. Just renew with adders.
Gold	Invest moderately more - Invest 5k 1st of every month
PF	No investments in PPF this year (max 10k)
Stocks	Invest more - a little moderately. Invest @ dips in all current stocks

Fig 40: *Guiding principles for investments in the coming year*

The guiding principles for investments that arose from this analysis are given below.

1. It was clear that I now needed to have a completely different strategy to invest in mutual funds. I needed to explore more options in mutual funds and also open new mutual fund accounts.

2. I needed to control or limit the investment in fixed deposits since they were giving me minimum returns and I had already invested a large sum in fixed deposits.

3. I needed to create a sort of SIP for my gold investments and continue to moderately invest in gold on a regular basis.

4. There was already a lot of money invested in PPF and EPF accounts and I needed to make absolutely sure that I did not block more in these accounts, except for the standard deductions made by the company.

5. Stocks were still the best bet and I knew I needed to continue to invest at dips in stocks to maximize my returns.

All these guidelines would not have been feasible had I not done this thorough analysis of my current portfolio till date.

With this, we have reached the end of our financial planning and tracking section. I sincerely hope it has given you some useful information, that you will be able to utilize and that my experience will benefit you.

I would recommend that you visit the website at

http//www.ratrace2freedom.com and check out the latest versions of various downloadable templates and calculators that are built in for your convenience.

Step 8: Celebrate milestones with your family

You have planned well and started your journey towards achieving one of the biggest things in life – your own freedom. Just as with any stock market fluctuation, this journey will have its own ups and downs, moments of cheer and excitement as well as moments of sadness and depression.

I heard a statement repeatedly while I was doing network marketing with Amway, which says: If your goals and dreams are big enough, facts don't count.

It is very true. It does not matter what your family income is today, whether you are unable to save as per the target you have set for yourself, whether you started too late or whether you started some time earlier in life and failed. It doesn't matter what your near and dear feel about your dream and goals. Nothing matters at all! The only thing that matters is what you feel about what you are trying to achieve and what you want to do once you have achieved financial freedom.

Your family and friends will join your journey when they understand it. I can tell you one thing for sure, the day they understand it, they will be your biggest supporters and in fact they will be the ones who will encourage you when you feel your goals are eluding you.

Remember that your close family sacrifices as much, if not more than you do. You are sacrificing because you have a definite goal and you know how to achieve it. Your family may not know and understand your goal, but still supports you, which must be duly appreciated.

To involve them in your goals, as well as to realize the importance of each step, you must make it a definite point to celebrate the intermediate milestones with your family. For example, I remember that during my journey towards my goal of a nest egg of 1.7 Crores (or 17 million), we celebrated every million that we reached with a party at home. The day when we touched the next million, we ordered pizzas, celebrated and had fun.

We still have pleasant memories of many of those achievements and with each such celebration, our family became more united and had more and more faith in my goal and aspirations.

So start as soon as you can, and make your journey as interesting, exciting and memorable as you can.

This is not an easy journey but is definitely worthwhile. If I have been able to do it, anyone can. As long as your dreams and goals are clear and are driving you, nothing is impossible.

Before we conclude the book, it was important that we take a quick look on some "little known" tax saving tips, as mentioned in the next section. These are some of the tips that most of us are usually unaware of. There are other standard ways to save taxes and you should refer to your financial advisor or online information for most recent updates on those.

But the tips in the next section will encourage you to delve deeper and gain more information about this from trusted and latest sources.

6

Saving on Taxes

A penny saved is a dollar earned.
*— **Benjamin Franklin***

We often tend to neglect the saving element in the portfolio and tend to focus most of our time and energy on the earning aspect. While earning more is important, savings is no less. As Benjamin Franklin wisely said – A penny saved is a dollar earned. For each dollar you earn, you save only a fraction of the amount but if you can save some money, it directly accumulates in your portfolio.

Often, one of the most neglected means of saving is the saving on taxes that are deducted at source. A lot can be done on this front with basic minimum awareness of tax laws.

The Income Tax Act 1961 is a voluminous piece of legislation. Taxmann Publications' latest edition of the act runs into 1,125 pages. This is enough to intimidate even the most diligent law student and tax expert, leave alone ordinary taxpayers like you and me. But hidden away in the 300-odd sections and 14 schedules are clauses that can benefit ordinary taxpayers-provided they know how to claim those benefits.

The phrase 'tax savings' brings to mind life insurance, Public Provident Fund, National Savings Certificate, and equity-linked savings schemes, among others, that qualify for tax deduction under Section 80 C of the Income-Tax Act. An individual can claim tax deductions of up to ₹ 1 lac under Section 80 C.

However, there are other lesser known avenues that offer additional tax breaks to individuals. They are not widely discussed as they involve special situations in life.

In this section we give some little-known tax benefits you may be entitled to, which can help you save tax over and above the tax saving investments you make during the year. These laws are true to the best of my knowledge at the time this book was being written. Income tax laws undergo frequent changes and this education must be a part of the ongoing "sharpen your financial saw" activity that you should pursue. These laws are by no means, explicit or elaborate.

Use losses in stocks to cut tax

Can you gain from the short-term losses you made on stocks? Yes, says the Income Tax Act. If you have made any long-term capital gains from the sale of property, gold or debt funds, you can offset them against short-term capital losses made on stocks and bring down your tax liability. "Short-term capital losses can be set off against both short-term capital gains as well as taxable long-term capital gains," says Sandeep Shanbhag, director of Wonderland Consultants, a Mumbai-based tax planning and financial consultancy.

This can be especially useful for someone who has booked profits on gold ETFs and physical gold. Suppose you have sold some property and made a long-term capital gain of ₹ 30 lacs after indexation.

At 20%, the tax payable on this long-term capital gain is ₹ 6 lacs. However, if you have also sold some junk stocks during the year and made a short-term loss of ₹ 3 lacs, you can set this off against the gains from the property. Then the gain from the property will be reduced to only ₹ 27 lacs and the tax payable will be ₹ 5.4 lacs.

However, the law makes a distinction here. One cannot set off short-term gains from stocks against long-term capital losses from the other assets. Long-term capital losses can only be set off against taxable long-term capital gains.

Get deduction for rent even without HRA

House rent can account for as much as 40-50% of total household expenses. This is why house rent allowance is exempt from tax up to a certain limit. But what if your salary does not include an HRA component or you are a self-employed professional or businessman? Under Section 80GG, you can claim deduction of the rent paid even if you do not get HRA. "Not many people are aware of this deduction," says chartered accountant Mehul Sheth. However, there are stiff conditions to be met. The least of the following three can be claimed as deduction: rent paid less 10% of total income; or ₹ 2,000 a month; or 25% of total income. Also, the taxpayer should not be drawing any HRA or any housing benefit.

Besides, the taxpayer and his/her spouse or minor child should not own a house in the city where he stays and he should not be claiming tax benefits for some other self-occupied house.

Invest as much as you can prior to tax deduction

The whole idea of your retirement saving schemes, whether they are a Public Provident Fund (PPF), Employee Provident Fund (EPF) or Voluntary Provident Fund (VPF) is that you save money during your younger years (when your income and salary are high) on taxes. Then you can withdraw the same funds when you are set to retire and your income is lower.

At that time, you may pay relatively very low taxes on your retirement fund withdrawals because of the low tax slabs that you may fall in at that stage. Thus you end up paying lower taxes when you withdraw during retirement than you would have paid when you were younger and working. In short, the government shifts the tax burden from the older persons to the younger persons.

Most of the withdrawals in the retirement schemes as above give you tax free principal and interest withdrawals.

There are other schemes which are prevalent from time to time, like investments in infrastructure bonds etc., where you can invest with tax exemptions and though your withdrawals may be taxed later, at that stage, you may fall in a lower tax bracket.

Paying rent to your parents

If you are staying in your parents' house, you can consider paying rent to them. This can help you save income tax if your parents fall in a lower tax bracket. However, note that it is advisable that you enter into an agreement with them and actually make the payment every month, preferably by cheque.

If your parents are retired and do not derive any significant taxable income, they can claim tax exemption on the rent you pay them. So, in effect, you are utilizing the lower tax slab of your parent's income to save tax on the house rent allowance.

Charity to noble causes

Charitable contributions, of up to 10% of your income, are deductible under Section 80G. Depending upon the institution to which the donation is being made, the deduction can be either 100% or 50% of the amount donated.

Ensure that you obtain a receipt from the institution and a copy of their income-tax exemption certificate. Instead of giving the money directly to the needy and not getting any deduction, you can make a charitable contribution to an NGO that provides assistance to the needy. The individual is then able to get a tax deduction while still contributing to a noble cause.

Home loans

The principal repayment of a home loan qualifies for deduction under section 80C; the interest payable on the home loan is allowed as deduction under section 24 of the act.

The deduction in respect of the interest is available in full for properties that are treated as let-out, but in case of a property treated as self-occupied, the amount cannot exceed ₹ 1.5 lacs per financial year, subject to certain conditions.

However, you cannot claim interest deduction when the flat is under construction. The interest paid during the pre-construction period can be claimed as a deduction in five equal installments starting from the financial year in which the construction is completed. Where the property is jointly owned, with the share of each owner being definite, the net taxable annual value of the property is apportioned to each of the joint owners in the ratio of their share in the property. And, as the shares are definite, each holder is eligible to claim a separate deduction in case the property is jointly owned.

Educational expenses for children

It is well-known that deduction under section 80C is available to an individual in respect of the tuition fees of his/her children with an overall limit of ₹ 1 lac. The deduction, however, is not available for capitation fees/donations collected by a school or college. There is another section in the act (section 80E) which provides for deduction in respect of interest on loans taken for higher education.

The educational loan can be taken for any course pursued by the individual or the spouse or children of the individual post the senior secondary course or its equivalent. This deduction is also available for supporting the education of a relative provided the individual is his/her legal guardian. It is allowed for a maximum of eight years starting from the year in which the interest is first repaid.

Many times during the course of my journey, I thought that I should now quit my job even though I knew I had not achieved my goal of financial freedom completely. Some of you may also feel the same way as you near your goals.

The next section will give you a quick glimpse of what you must definitely do before you finally quit your job.

7

Before Calling It a Day

I don't dream at night, I dream all day;
I dream for a living.
— **Steven Spielberg**

A mediocre idea that generates enthusiasm will go
further than a great idea that inspires no one.
— **Mary K Ash**

Sooner or later, and I am sure when you are very close to your financial freedom plan, you will reach a day when you think you have accumulated enough money in your nest egg. You will feel that you have accumulated so much money that the money can now take care of itself, just like a grown up child whom you nourished, cared for and helped reach a certain stage in life where he or she can take care of him/herself. Not only that, just like your grown up child, money can now take care of you as well. You have crossed that threshold amount which is needed for the money to actually act as your slave, and create more money automatically without working.

You are finally at the doorstep of financial independence. Let me assure that this is by no means a small achievement. Less than 2% of the world's population dream of achieving this and less than 1% actually achieve it.

You are now at a stage where you are not compelled to work for anyone, unless of course you enjoy doing so. You now have the freedom to do what you want to do.

I often compare financial freedom with the independence of a nation. There is no denying the fact that the most important day in the life of a nation is when the nation became independent. We celebrate that day with joy and enthusiasm every year. Why? What is so special about independence? Were we not able to survive without being independent? We were. Then what is so important about being independent? The answer is that an independent nation can decide its own path, it can decide what is good and not so good for its people, what policies it wants to follow, what its goals are, etc...Human nature is such that people get happiness and joy when they can act and do what they really want to do.

The same holds true with financial independence. We have been a free nation for last 65 years but the more important question is whether we are free as human beings? Are we doing what we really enjoy doing in life? That enjoyment could come from helping others, spending every day with your children and seeing them grow up, doing something worthwhile to improve society, the country or the world, or it could be as simple as chasing your dreams of writing a book, being a professional guitar player, exploring the world, going for adventure trips....

Most of us are unable to do all these things because we have a job to go to or we have a business commitment. If you really do not enjoy doing what you are doing and are compelled to do so because you have to earn money, then you are still a slave looking for that elusive independence. You need to come out of the rat race and look for bigger and worthwhile things in life.

Once you achieve financial freedom you can enjoy doing what you always wanted to do. Some of you may get over excited and quit your job having reached your financial goals. However, it is wise to be cautious, as there are certain important things to be kept in mind before you finally call it a day.

Life and health insurance

Keep yourself and your family protected during this journey. Remember that you are not financially secure till you have completed the journey and therefore, both life and health insurance cover is important for you and your family.

Normally, if you were in a job, your organization would have covered you for your and your family's health insurance through the company's group insurance policy. The premium of such a group insurance policy is normally deducted from your salary automatically.

Since you will not be employed post your financial independence, it is extremely important that you and your family are adequately covered through a private health insurance provider before you quit your job and your company group insurance policy lapses.

Retirement benefits

To get the best retirement benefits, it is advisable to collect the latest information and all details of the persons who deal with provident funds, gratuity and superannuation schemes; HR contacts, email addresses, phone numbers, addresses etc., of the key contacts within your company so that once you leave, it is not difficult for you to follow up on your benefits.

8

Go for It!

Never give up. You only get one life. Go for it!
— **Richard E. Grant**

Now that we have come to the end of the book, I would like to conclude by giving you a few success pills that will help you in shaping and cruising through your own journey successfully. You have to do your own thinking and chart your own way. My journey was my way of handling my investments. You may follow the same path or you may define a path that works best for you.

KISS

KISS stands for 'Keep It Simple, Stupid.' Financial terms and jargon can appear to be complex and intimidating at times. However, let me assure you once again that you do not need anything more than a logical mind to figure out what is happening around you, and then take appropriate decisions of your own to learn and earn as you progress.

Let us take the example of life insurance. There are innumerable products available in the market today that can confuse you on where to invest and how much to invest so that you are financially secure as well as get returns on your investments.

If you keep things simple, the first fundamental question is: Why do you need to insure yourself? The answer is: So that your loved ones and dependents can enjoy the same quality of life even after you are not around. Therefore, for life insurance, you need a product that provides exactly this – term insurance.Why mix insurance with investment? Why complicate things when you can keep them simple?

As long as you keep things simple and trust your own judgment based on your own knowledge, you will always be better off in the long run.

Trust me, you need freedom

Once, when I was on my weekly shopping expedition, with my family, at an Indian grocery, I met one of my colleagues in the store. Not that there was anything special about meeting a colleague, but that day he seemed very disturbed and perturbed about something. On enquiry I learnt that his father had been detected with cancer. Not only was it an emotional shock for him, but he was also aware of the financial implications. His father would have to undergo a series of chemotherapy treatments for at least a year, before his prognosis would be realistically known.

I still remember the moment when I put my hand on his shoulder, looked into his eyes and told him that if he needed any kind of financial help, I would be ever willing to help. The moment I uttered these words, I felt very satisfied. I am telling you this because like most of you, I have faced similar situations in my life but I never had the means to openly offer any kind of financial help to anyone, even though I wanted to offer. I was always worried about my own future and that of my immediate family.

For me, this was a massive shift in the way I used to think and in the very purpose of my existence. I was moving from asking for help or being self sufficient at best, to being "able to help others". If you have never experienced such a feeling, you will not realize how satisfied you feel when you are in a position to offer such help to anyone. It is this feeling of freedom to help anyone that in itself is enough to drive you to the changes that you need to achieve your personal financial freedom.

God knows how to help you

If your intentions are good, God will always find a way to help you achieve your goals. Have trust, keep trying and things will surely fall into place. I want to give you a personal example. During my journey of financial freedom, in the year 2012, my target to achieve my monthly goals increased by around ₹ 50,000 per month, from what it was in 2011. I did not know how to achieve this additional ₹ 50,000 per month. I knew that around 25% of this additional amount could be covered by the monthly interest generated from the nest egg that I had at the end of 2011, but I did not know from where I was to get the remaining 75%. I was determined to achieve my goals but I had no idea how I would be able to do so.

On 2nd Jan 2012 – the first working day of the year in office - three things happened within 3 hours, which proved to me that God knows how to help you.

- ▶ *6:30 a.m* - I checked the stock market and for the first time my portfolio had increased by almost 15% in one day whereas it had decreased by almost 50% through 2011.

- ▶ *7:30 a.m* – Before leaving for office, I checked my mail box and quite unbelievably, I found a $100 refund from my dentist whom I had visited some 4 months back. Not that $100 was a big amount but it was completely unexpected and most welcome.

- ▶ *8:30 a.m* – In office whilst going through the mails, flashes a mail from my manager in India which states that my salary has been increased by more than 10% as a special off cycle promotion. This "off cycle" progression was again unexpected (it is not a normal annual salary increment) and had never happened to me before in my 17 year long career.

- ▸ Not only that, a few other things happened around this time period which further strengthened my belief that nature, universe and God were conspiring to help me achieve my goals.

- ▸ I was earning my salary in US dollars and was able to transfer money to India online. After we reached the US (early in the year 2010), the US dollar appreciated heavily against the rupee, breaking all previous records. From ₹ 44, the price of one USD rose to ₹ 53. This in itself was a 20% jump in the money that I was earning in the US. The dollar continued to stay high and I took full advantage of this appreciation by transferring most of my money to India at a higher exchange rate.

- ▸ I received a cash award in my January 2012 salary slip, which till today, is an unknown element. I do not know from where it came and why, and that too at a time when there are no cash rewards as per company policy these days.

With all this, by mid January 2012, I was sure of how to get the additional ₹ 50,000 per month. It proved to me once again that if one really wants to achieve something, the entire universe conspires to make it happen. The teachings from the books, *The Alchemist* and *The Secret* were coming true. I was certain that God existed and that He is helping me achieve my goals.

Trust me, the same will happen with you. So, do not ever abandon your goals. You will find a way out of a difficult situation or a demanding target if you keep trying with the right intentions. Things around you will change in a way that will help you to achieve your goals.

Nurture your nest egg

As and when you retire, which I am sure you will, you may leave your job or small business and focus on how to continue to nurture your nest egg. One of the most important things that will make sure that you take the right decisions to nourish your portfolio is sharpening your financial saw. I still read more than 10 to 15 articles everyday on the economic situation around me so that I can take informed decisions.

You must always make sure that you continue to beat inflation by acquiring the right knowledge and applying that knowledge to invest wisely. It will be easier to do that now since you are not dependent on your income anymore and have learnt the rules of the game.

So now it is up to you and I wish you all the best for your journey.

Last but not least I want to see you succeed. If you need help, feel free to visit the website,http://www.ratrace2freedom.com and look for solutions, or email me and I will try and respond and help you.

Wishing you true freedom!

Glossary

1. Financial Freedom
The freedom to choose what you want to do and how you want to shape your life is financial freedom. It comes when all financial constraints are lifted and you move towards real and pleasurable goals.

2. Millionaire
An individual whose net worth or wealth is equal to or exceeds one million units of currency. It can also be a person who owns one million units of currency in a bank account or savings account. Depending on the currency, a certain level of prestige is associated with being a millionaire, which makes that amount of wealth a goal for some, and almost unattainable for others.

3. Financial Independence
Same as (1) Financial Freedom

4. Good Financial Practices (GFP)
Habits, personal traits and financial discipline, that stimulate wealth accumulation over time.

5. Rat Race
It is defined as an endless, self-defeating or pointless pursuit. It conjures up an image of the futile efforts of a lab rat trying to escape while running around a maze or in a wheel. In an analogy to the modern city, many rats in a single maze expend a lot of effort running around, but ultimately achieve nothing (meaningful) either collectively or individually.

6. Equity Market (Stock Market)
A stock market or equity market is a public entity (a loose network of economic transactions, not a physical facility or discrete entity) for trading company stock (shares) and derivatives at an agreed price.

7. Financially Stable
Someone who can continue to make ends meet without a great deal of stress or difficulty can be termed as financially stable. Financial stability is different from financial freedom. Such a person has just enough money to manage his or her self and the immediate family.

8. Investment
The process of putting money into something with the expectation of gain, which upon thorough analysis, has a high degree of security for the principal amount, as well as security of return, within an expected period of time.

9. Asset
Anything tangible or intangible that is capable of being owned or controlled and has a positive economic value-add for the owner. An asset pays the owner.

10. Liability
Anything tangible or intangible that is capable of being owned or controlled and has a negative economic value-add for the owner. An owner pays for the liability.

11. Net Worth (Book Value)
Net worth is defined as the total assets minus total liabilities of an individual or a company. For a company, this is referred to as book value.

12. Barter System
Barter is a method of exchange by which goods or services are directly exchanged for other goods or services without using a medium of exchange, such as money.

13. Commodity
A commodity is the generic term for any marketable item produced to satisfy wants or needs e.g., copper, aluminium, petroleum, pulses etc.

14. Derivative
A derivative is anything that is derived from something which is more tangible. For example, apple juice is a derivative of an apple or wood is a derivative of a tree. In

financial terms, any currency like the Dollar or Rupee is a derivative of gold.

15. Inflation
Inflation is a rise in the general level of prices of goods and services in an economy over a period of time. When the general price level rises, each unit of currency buys fewer goods and services. Consequently, Inflation reflects erosion in the purchasing power of money.

16. Central Bank (Reserve Bank)
A Central Bank is a public institution that manages the nation's currency, money supply, and interest rates. Central banks also usually oversee the commercial banking system of their respective countries e.g., The Reserve Bank of India or Federal Reserve of the United States.

17. Returns or Return on Investments (ROI)
Returns on Investments is one way of considering profits in relation to capital invested.

18. Absolute Returns
Absolute returns are a measure of the gain or loss on an investment portfolio expressed as a percentage of invested capital. It has no relation to the time for which the investment was made or to the interest received during the invested period.

19. Simple Annual ROI
It provides an annualized version of the returns on investment.

20. Interest
The charge for the privilege of borrowing money, typically expressed as an annual percentage rate. Interest is commonly calculated using one of two methods: simple interest calculation, or compound interest calculation. Lenders make money from interest, borrowers pay it.

21. CAGR (Compounded Annual Growth Rate)
This method of calculation where the interest earned is re-invested for a future tenure and contributes to the overall returns is called Compounded Annual Growth Rate (or CAGR).

22. Principal
The amount borrowed or the amount still owed on a loan, separate from interest. Also known as the original amount invested, separate from earnings.

23. IRR (Internal Rate of Return) or Discounted Cash Flow Rate Of Return (DFCOR)
IRR is a rate of return used in capital budgeting to measure and compare the profitability of investments. The term internal refers to the fact that its calculation does not incorporate environmental factors (e.g., the interest rate or inflation).

24. SIP (Systematic Investment Plan)
This is a plan where investors make regular, equal payments into a mutual fund, trading account, retirement account or any other investment accounts. By using a systematic investment plan, investors benefit from the long-term advantages of dollar-cost averaging and the convenience of saving regularly without taking any actions except the initial setup of the SIP.

25. Cost Inflation Index (CII)
RBI publishes an inflation number called the Cost Inflation Index every year. The Cost Inflation Index in itself does not convey anything but the increase in the number from one year to another is representative of the change in prices (and therefore, inflation) between these years.

26. Tax
To tax is the imposition of a financial charge or other levy upon a

taxpayer by a state, or the functional equivalent of a state, such that failure to pay is punishable by law.

27. **Taxpayer**
A taxpayer is an individual or a legal entity that pays taxes.

28. **Income Tax**
Income tax is a tax levied on the income of individuals or businesses (corporations or other legal entities).

29. **Capital Gain**
A capital gain is a profit that results from investments into a capital asset, such as stocks, bonds or real estate, which exceeds the purchase price. It is the difference between a higher selling price and a lower purchase price, resulting in a financial gain for the investor.

30. **Capital Asset**
Assets used to make money, as opposed to assets used for personal enjoyment or consumption e.g., stocks, bonds or real estate.

31. **Dollar Cost Averaging (DCA)**
It is an investment strategy that may be used with any currency. It takes the form of investing equal monetary amounts regularly and periodically over specific time periods (such as $100 per month) in a particular investment or portfolio. By doing so, more shares are purchased when prices are low and fewer shares are purchased when prices are high. The point of this is to lower the total average cost per share of the investment, giving the investor a lower overall cost for the shares purchased over time.

32. **Rule of 72**
It is a method for estimating the time it will take for an investment to double. The rule number is divided by the interest percentage per period to obtain the approximate number of periods (usually years) required for doubling. For example, money

earning a 10% annual interest will double in 72/10 = 7.2 years.

33. **Portfolio**
Portfolio literally means a "case for carrying loose papers". In our context, it is a collection of investments held by an investment company, hedge fund, financial institution or individual.

34. **Asset Classes**
A way to classify assets based on the risk reward ratio and the investment types.

35. **Asset Class Category**
Further sub categorization of asset classes is done through asset class categories, e.g., large-cap stocks or short-term bonds.

36. **Equity**
Equity is the value of an ownership interest in property, including shareholders' equity in a business.

37. **Risk**
Risk is the potential that a chosen action or activity (including the choice of inaction) will lead to a loss (an undesirable outcome).

38. **Risk Appetite**
This is the level of risk that an individual or an organization is prepared to accept, before action is deemed necessary to reduce the risk.

39. **Portfolio Asset Allocation or Asset Allocation**
Asset allocation is an investment strategy that attempts to balance risk versus reward by adjusting the percentage of each asset in an investment portfolio according to the investors risk tolerance, goals and investment time frame.

40. **Nest Egg**
The accumulated target amount that triggers key goals e.g., the total amount required to be accumulated to trigger financial freedom.

41. **Fixed Deposit or Term Deposit or Time Deposit**
Fixed deposits are a kind of high-interest-yielding deposit offered by banks in India.

42. **Bank**
A bank is a financial institution and a financial intermediary that accepts deposits and channels those deposits into lending activities, either directly or through capital markets. A bank connects customers with capital deficits to customers with capital surpluses.

43. **Base Lending Rate**
It is the rate at which banks borrow money from the Reserve Bank of India or other similar central banks in their respective countries. Banks lend this money to their customers and earn from the interest on that money.

44. **Reserve Bank of India (RBI)**
The central bank for India is the Reserve Bank of India.

45. **Recurring Deposit**
Recurring deposits are a special kind of term deposits offered by banks in India which help people with regular incomes to deposit a fixed amount every month into their recurring deposit account and earn interest at the rate applicable to fixed deposits.

46. **Tax Deduction at Source (TDS)**
TDS is one of the modes of collecting income tax from assesses in India. This is governed under the Indian Income Tax Act, 1961, by the Central Board for Direct Taxes (CBDT). As the name suggests, tax is deducted at the source of income generation i.e. at the time of salary disbursement.

47. **Public Provident Fund (PPF)**
Public Provident Fund (PPF) is a savings-cum-tax saving instrument in India. It also serves as a retirement planning tool for many of those who do not have any structured pension plan covering them.

48. **Lock in Period**
It is the time period for which the investment is blocked and cannot be withdrawn or re-invested.

49. **Employee Provident Fund (EPF) or PF**
It is a compulsory investment for all salaried people (if you work for a company having 20 or more employees). It is a long-term and one of the lowest risk investment avenues, as it is backed by the government

50. **EPF Office (EPFO)**
It is a statutory body of the Government of India under the Ministry of Labour and Employment. It administers a compulsory contributory provident fund scheme, pension scheme and an insurance scheme. It is one of the largest social security organizations in the world in terms of the number of covered beneficiaries and the volume of financial transactions undertaken.

51. **Voluntary Provident Fund (VPF)**
VPF is the additional contribution to an EPF account over and above the mandatory contribution.

52. **Section 80C**
While exemptions are on income, some deduction in calculation of taxable income is allowed for certain payments. Section 80C of the Income Tax Act allows certain investments and expenditure to be deducted from total income up to a maximum of 1 Lac.

53. **Gratuity**
Literally, gratuity means "tip". This is one of the additional retirement benefits that are available to the Indian salaried class.

54. Superannuation

In general, a pension is an arrangement to provide people with an income when they are no longer earning a regular income from employment. The terms "retirement plan" or "superannuation" refer to a pension granted upon retirement.

55. Exchange Traded Funds

An Exchange Traded Fund (ETF) is an investment fund traded on stock exchanges, much like stocks. An ETF holds assets such as stocks, commodities or bonds, and trades close to its net asset value over the course of the trading day. Most ETFs track an index, such as the S&P 500, Nifty 500, and Gold ETF etc. ETFs may be attractive as investments because of their low costs, tax efficiency and stock-like features. By owning an ETF, you get the diversification of an index fund as well as the ability to sell short, buy on margin and purchase as little as one share.

56. Bullion Market

Bullion is defined as a bulk quantity of precious metals consisting of gold, silver and other metals that can be assessed by weight and cast as a lump. Bullion is valued by its purity and mass rather than its face value which is applicable in the case of money. The bullion reserve of a country is the indicator of the amount of wealth a country possesses.

57. Dematerialized

Dematerialized or "Demat" means to "deprive of" or lose the physical substance or make or become immaterial. In our context, dematerialization is a process in which you can convert physical share certificates into electronic shares. The shares should have been transferred in your name before sending them for dematerialization.

58. Debt

A debt is an obligation owed by one party (the debtor) to a second party (the creditor). A debt is created when a creditor agrees to lend a sum of assets to a debtor. Debt is usually granted with expected repayment; in modern society, in most cases, of the original sum plus interest.

59. Equity

Equity is a stock or any other security representing an ownership interest. In the context of real estate, it is the amount that the owner would receive after selling a property and paying off the mortgage.

60. Initial Public Offering (IPO)

The first sale of stock by a private company to the general public is through an Initial Public Offering (IPO). IPOs are often issued by smaller, younger companies seeking the capital to expand, but can also be issued by large privately owned companies looking to become publicly traded. IPOs can be a risky investment. For the individual investor, it is difficult to predict how a stock will fare on its initial day of trading and in the near future because there is often little historical data with which to analyze the company. Also, most IPOs are of companies going through a transitory growth period, which are subject to additional uncertainty regarding their future values.

61. Stock Exchange

Same as (6) – Equity market/Stock market

62. Price to Earnings Ratio (P/E Ratio)

It is a measure of the price paid for a share relative to the annual profit earned by the firm per share. The P/E ratio can therefore alternatively be calculated by dividing the company's market capitalization by its total annual earnings.

63. Earnings Per Share (EPS)

Earnings Per Share (EPS) are the amount of earnings per each outstanding share of a company's stock.

64. Dividend

Dividends are payments made by a corporation to its shareholder members. It is the portion of corporate profits paid out to stockholders.

65. Dividend Payout Ratio

Dividend payout ratio is the fraction of net income a firm pays to its stockholders in dividends. The part of the earnings not paid to investors is left for investment to provide for future earnings growth.

66. Profit After Tax (PAT)

PAT is the net profit earned by the company after deducting all expenses like interest, depreciation and tax. PAT can be fully retained by a company to be used in the business. Dividends, if declared, are paid to the share holders from this residue.

67. Dividend Yield

A financial ratio that shows how much a company pays out in dividends each year relative to its share price. In the absence of any capital gains, the dividend yield is the return on investment for a stock.

68. Demat Account

An account holding shares in a dematerialized form. Such an account, normally, also allows transactions of shares.

69. DP or Depository Participant

Depository Participant (DP) is described as an agent of the depository. They are the intermediaries between the depository and the investors. The relationship between the DPs and the depository is governed by an agreement made between the two under the Depositories Act. In a strictly legal sense, a DP is an entity who is registered as such with SEBI.

70. Securities

A security is generally a negotiable financial instrument representing financial value. Securities are broadly categorized into debt securities (such as banknotes, bonds and debentures), equity securities, e.g., common stocks; and derivative contracts, such as forwards, futures, options and swaps.

71. Bonds

Certificates that represent money a government or corporation has borrowed from other entities like the public.

72. Credit Rating

A credit rating evaluates the credit worthiness of an issuer of specific types of debt, specifically, debt issued by a business enterprise such as a corporation or a government. It is an evaluation made by a credit rating agency of the debt issuer's likelihood of default. Credit ratings are determined by credit ratings agencies.

73. Credit Advisors or Credit Rating Agencies

A credit rating agency is a company that assigns credit ratings to issuers of certain types of debt obligations as well as the debt instruments themselves.

74. Mutual Funds

A mutual fund is a professionally managed type of collective investment scheme that pools money from many investors to buy stocks, bonds, short-term money market instruments, and/or other securities

75. Net Assets Value (NAV)

An NAV is a mutual fund's price per share or exchange-traded fund's (ETF) per-share value. In both cases, the per-share dollar amount of the fund is calculated by dividing the total value of all the securities in its portfolio, less any liabilities, by the number of fund shares outstanding.

76. Portfolio Manager
A portfolio manager is either a person who makes investment decisions using money other people have placed under his or her control or a person who manages a financial institution's asset and liability (loan and deposit) portfolios. A portfolio manager is very common in mutual funds.

77. Fixed Maturity Plans (FMPs)
Fixed Maturity Plans (FMPs) are close ended mutual fund debt schemes that have a predetermined maturity date. They predominantly invest in government securities, corporate debt, commercial papers and money market instruments and aim at generating steady returns over a fixed period.

78. Close Ended Funds
It is a collective investment scheme with a limited number of shares. It is called a Closed End Fund (CEF) because new shares are rarely issued once the fund has been launched, and because shares are not normally redeemable for cash or securities until the fund liquidates.

79. Commodities
Same as (13).

80. Life Insurance
Life insurance is a contract between an insurance policy holder and an insurer, where the insurer promises to pay a designated beneficiary a sum of money (the "benefits") upon the death of the insured person.

81. Insurance Premium
The insurer charges a premium to be paid upfront or in instalments, in exchange for a certain type and amount of coverage for a specified time period.

82. Real Estate
Real estate is property consisting of land and the buildings on it, along with its natural resources such as crops, minerals, or water; or any other immovable property of this nature.

83. First Generation Millionaires
First generation millionaires are those millionaires who earned their money on their own. Many millionaires simply worked, saved, and lived within their means to generate their wealth.

84. Net Worth
Same as (11).

85. Assets
Same as (9).

86. Liabilities
Same as (10).

87. Liquidate
Liquidation is the process by which a company (or part of a company) is brought to an end, and the assets and property of the company redistributed.

88. PAN
Permanent Account Number (PAN) is unique alphanumeric combination issued to all juristic entities identifiable under the Indian Income Tax Act 1961. It is issued by the Indian Income Tax Department

89. Know Your Customer (KYC)
With effect from 1st January 2011, any investor (all applicants in a folio) investing into mutual funds through the Investment Services Account would be required to be KYC compliant with CVL(CDSL Ventures Ltd) without which the transactions may be liable to be rejected by the respective mutual fund houses.

90. Fractional Reserve
A fractional reserve indicates the fraction of the money receipts issued

by a bank for which it physically holds commodities. For example, a 3:1 fractional reserve indicates that the bank is allowed to issue or lend ₹ 300 worth of money in case it physically holds ₹ 100 worth of commodities.

Fractional reserve ratios have increased in modern times allowing banks to loan much more money than they actually have. This leads to typical modern day situations in which the loan takers may default and depositors start asking for their money, leading to the banks going bankrupt.

REFERENCES &
RECOMMENDATIONS

Recommended Books

- Rhonda Byrne. *The Secret*
- Robert T. Kiyosaki. *Rich Dad Poor Dad*
- Thomas Stanley. *The Millionaire Next Door*
- Robert T. Kiyosaki. *Rich Dad's Conspiracy of the Rich*
- Investopedia (http://www.investopedia.com)
- George S. Clayson. *The Richest Man in Babylon*
- Daniel R. Solin. *The Smartest Retirement Book You Will Ever Read*
- Bambi Holzer. *Retire Rich*
- RaagVamDatt (http://www.raagvamdatt.com)
- Suze Orman. *The 9 Steps to Financial Freedom*
- Suze Orman. *The Laws of Money, The Lessons of Life*
- Charles Schwab. *New Guide to Financial Independence*
- Jim Taylor, Doug Harrison, Stephen Kraus. *The New Elite*
- Douglas R. Andrew. *The Last Chance Millionaire*
- Stephen R. Covey. *The Seven Habits of Highly Effective People*
- Seth Godin. *Retirement Planning*
- Don Underwood. *Grow Rich Slowly*
- Richard Paul Evans. *The Five Lessons a Millionaire Taught Me About Life and Wealth*
- Jane Bryant Quinn. *Smart & Simple Financial Strategies for Busy People*

Recommended Movies

▶ In Front of Class (English)

An inspirational movie about never losing sight of your dream in spite of any challenges that you may face in life.

▶ Ta Ra Rum Pum (Hindi)

A family entertainment movie on the importance of why it is more important to "save more" rather than "earn more".

▶ Chak De India (Hindi)

A family entertainment sports movie on how to team up for success. It teaches us that nothing is impossible when you dream big.